Wagner

For Oliver and Abigail

Cover design and art direction by Pearce Marchbank Studio
Cover photography by Julian Hawkins

Printed and bound in the United Kingdom by
Dotesios Printers Ltd., Trowbridge, Wiltshire

© Howard Gray 1990
Published in 1990 by Omnibus Press, a division of Book Sales Limited

Although efforts have been made to trace the present copyright holders of photographs, the publishers apologise in advance for any unintentional omission or neglect and will be pleased to insert the appropriate acknowledgement to companies or individuals in any subsequent edition of this book.

Hardback
Order No. OP44940
ISBN 0.7119.1629.2

Softback
Order No. OP44817
ISBN 0.7119.1687.X

Exclusive Distributors:
Book Sales Limited,
8/9 Frith Street,
London W1V 5TZ,
England.
Music Sales Pty Limited,
120 Rothschild Avenue,
Rosebery,
NSW 2018,
Australia.
To The Music Trade Only:
Music Sales Limited,
8/9 Frith Street,
London W1V 5TZ,
England.
Music Sales Corporation,
225 Park Avenue South,
New York,
N.Y. 10003,
U.S.A.

The Illustrated Lives of the Great Composers.

Wagner

Howard Gray

Omnibus Press
London/New York/Sydney

The Complete Series

Contents

1 Europe at War

By 1813, the year of Richard Wagner's birth, a momentous chapter in Europe's history was drawing to a close. The forces of change unleashed by the French Revolution had jolted the old order into a quarter of a century of intense social and political upheaval, with the figure of one man, Napoleon, dominating the war-scarred Continent with his military genius and Caesarist ambitions. Fuelled by his burning desire for power, Napoleon spread many of the ideas of the Revolution into a Europe still labouring under feudalism and antiquated territorial divisions, and brought almost every European power within the French orbit. Allied to other influences, such as industrialisation and population growth, which were already beginning to change the face of the nineteenth century, the struggle of the European nations to free themselves from Napoleon's tyranny was to have immeasurable consequences in determining the future of modern Europe.

Napoleon proclaimed himself Emperor in 1804 (causing Beethoven to strike out the dedication page of his *Eroica* symphony) and during the next decade he attempted to hammer western Europe into one subservient bloc of satellite territories, either by military conquest or diplomatic coups. In particular, he was intent on rivalling British supremacy, but after Nelson destroyed the French fleet at the Battle of Trafalgar in 1805, it was clear that Britain would remain superior at sea. Resorting to economic warfare, Napoleon introduced the Continental System to seal Europe against British trade, but this only had the effect of stiffening her resistance and throwing more of Europe into active hostility.

Eventually, the other great European powers came to realise that, in order to protect their separate interests, a combined effort was needed to defeat Napoleon. The Peninsular War of 1808, in which Spanish guerilla fighters, backed by the British navy, inflicted heavy losses on the French forces, signalled the

Meeting of Napoleon and Francis II, the last Holy Roman Emperor.

7

beginning of open revolt within the Empire. This was quickly followed by a costly campaign against Austria, concluded by the Battle of Wagram in 1809 which, although a victory for Napoleon, demonstrated that the balance of military power in Europe was evening up.

However, by far the greatest potential threat came from Russia, as the unstable French-Russian alliance began, inevitably, to crumble. Tsar Alexander refused to co-operate in the trade blockade of Britain and this, together with the Polish question, led Napoleon, in June 1812, to lead his Grand Army across the Niemen river and into Russia – a colossal error of judgement that Hitler was to repeat 130 years later. The Battle of Borodino left the road to Moscow open to Napoleon, but it proved to be a pyrrhic victory. French losses had been heavy and soon disease, desertion, and the impossible logistics of the campaign forced Napoleon to

Battle of the Nations, Leipzig.

At Leipzig, Napoleon suffered one of his greatest defeats.

order a retreat back to the Niemen. By the end of the march, through a devastated countryside frozen hard by the fearsome Russian winter, Napoleon had lost 250,000 men and his downfall was sealed.

As the news reached Europe, there was a universal stirring of national sentiment which rapidly took the form of widespread resistance. Friedrich Wilhelm III of Prussia joined forces with Russia, and drove Napoleon back to the west of the river Elbe in Germany; and after armistice talks with Chancellor Metternich finally broke down, Austria joined the allies and declared war in June 1813. Remarkably, Napoleon began with another victory, at Dresden, but diplomacy continued to work against him. By skilful manoeuvring, Metternich persuaded most of the States of the Confederation of the Rhine to join the allies – one notable exception being Saxony, whose king never wavered in his support for Napoleon. With the allies growing in strength, Napoleon's position at Dresden soon became untenable and he fell back again, to Leipzig, where he was to suffer one of his greatest defeats.

Leipzig was the most important city in Saxony at that time, a centre of commerce, learning and the arts, with especially long traditions in bookselling and publishing. Its international trade fairs had been famous since the middle ages, attracting thousands of visitors every year. Proud of its cultural and intellectual heritage, Leipzig distanced itself from the courtly tastes and fashions of Dresden, the capital, favoured by the Saxon nobility for its cosmopolitan elegance and architectural splendour. Leipzig could also boast notable buildings, however, including the university and the Church of St Thomas, both built in the fifteenth century and, of course, Auerbach's Keller, the inn which provided the setting for the student scene in Goethe's *Faust*.

The Battle of the Nations – one of the bloodiest and most decisive battles of the Napoleonic wars – began outside Leipzig on 16 October 1813. The fighting raged for three days, spreading into the city, until the streets were filled with the bodies of the dead and wounded. Napoleon lost 50,000 men, the broken fragments of his heavily outnumbered army forced to fall back to the Rhine. With the hospitals at Leipzig unable to accommodate all the casualties, disease soon took hold of the city, and thousands of citizens died in the ensuing typhus epidemic. One of the victims was Friedrich Wagner, registrar at Leipzig police headquarters. He was forty-four, and left a wife and eight children, the youngest of which, then only six months old, had been christened that August, and named Wilhelm Richard.

Napoleon.

10

2 Early Childhood

Richard Wagner was born in Leipzig on 22 May 1813, in the House of the Red and White Lion in Der Bruhl Street. His forebears had been established in Saxony since the mid-seventeenth century, all leading relatively unremarkable careers, mainly as schoolmasters or public servants. None had shown any exceptional musical talent, though his father, Friedrich (by all accounts an exotic character who enjoyed considerable popularity in Leipzig social circles), had an abiding passion for amateur theatricals – and, it seems, for some of the young actresses of the day, as young Wagner gathered from his mother's rueful recollections.

Through his interest in the theatre, Friedrich met a young actor, painter and poet named Ludwig Geyer, whom he took under his wing and encouraged to take up a professional acting career. The two became firm friends and Geyer became a regular visitor to the Wagner household, where he was to strike up a special affinity with Wagner's mother, Johanna. Nine months after Friedrich's death, Geyer married Johanna and thus became, until his death in 1821, the only father Wagner ever knew. Indeed, the boy was called Richard Geyer at school until he was almost fifteen, reverting to the name Wagner in 1828. Geyer's relationship with Johanna, stretching back several years before Friedrich's death, has given rise to continuing speculation concerning Wagner's paternity, with the possibility raised that Geyer was in fact Wagner's true father. The mystery has been fuelled by Wagner's own uncertainties on the subject and, like many events in his life, made more confusing by the unreliability of his autobiographical writings.

Throughout his life Wagner felt the need to revise and reinterpret his past, and the question of his paternity exercised him to a growing degree in later years, possibly as his anti-semitism grew more virulent (there was a suggestion that Geyer had Jewish blood). Wagner's second wife, Cosima, recorded in

Der Brühl, Leipzig.

her diaries in December 1868, that he 'did not believe' that Geyer was his real father, but he often wrote about 'my father Geyer'; and as late as 1870 was referring to the 'complete self-sacrifice' shown by Geyer in taking on the responsibility of looking after an impecunious widow and her large brood – as if it were 'expiation for some guilt'.

Advocates of Geyer also point to the extraordinary journey undertaken by Johanna and two-month-old Richard in July 1813 to visit Geyer in Teplitz in Bohemia. One explanation of this dangerous, hundred-mile trek through enemy-occupied territory could be that Johanna was anxious to show the baby to his natural father; a colourful scenario rather belied by the fact that Teplitz was probably safer at that time than Leipzig, the centre of growing military activity in the area. Also, there is not a scrap of evidence that Johanna consummated her relationship with Geyer while her

12

Wagner's mother, Johanna.

Wagner's mother, Johanna.

Ludwig Geyer.

husband was still alive and, although Wagner could have inherited his love of the theatre from either of his putative fathers, his abnormally large head and small body was a particular Wagner family trait.

A psychologist might be tempted to interpret the course of Wagner's life, his arrogance and egotism, and the many inner contradictions of his personality, in the light of an identity crisis arising from his 'dual' paternity, or from the emotional trauma of losing two fathers by the age of eight. Certainly, his unstable beginnings led Wagner, later in life, to romanticise freely – and often inaccurately – about the events of his early years; but there is no reason to doubt that he enjoyed a happy childhood and had, in Ludwig Geyer, a responsive and intelligent stepfather who was particularly fond of the boy and had great ambitions for him.

In August 1814, when Wagner was just over a year old, his

mother and Geyer married and the family moved to Dresden, where Geyer, as well as being engaged by the court theatre, was in demand as a portrait painter by such esteemed patrons as the Saxon royal family. The Geyer household enjoyed a reasonable standard of living, with Johanna very much the ruling, matriarchal figure in the hospitable house in the Moritzstrasse; and in February 1815 a child, Cäcilie, was born to them, just six months after their marriage. Wagner described his mother as 'a remarkable woman in the eyes of all who knew her', and throughout his life he retained a deep affection for her, his letters full of expressions of love and gratitude; and, subsequently, he acknowledged her influence on his art. His mother represented tenderness and security, and this is the role assigned to motherhood in his operas, notably in *Siegfried*. In the scene where the hero, stretched out under the linden tree, pays tribute to a mother's love ('Ah, how a son longs to see his mother!'), there are echoes of the isolation, and even guilt, Wagner felt after his mother was laid to rest one wintry February morning in 1848.

Like Wagner's paternity, an aura of mystery surrounds his mother's parentage. Johanna (née Patz) was officially the daughter of a master baker from Weissenfels, near Leipzig, though she was possibly the illegitimate daughter of Prince Constantine of Saxe-Weimar who, she claimed, paid for her education at one of Leipzig's top schools. Whatever the truth of this, it is clear that she was not well educated, but she made up for her lack of academic attainment with many other more human qualities, such as common sense, understanding and a keen sense of humour. Wagner later admitted that the strain of bringing up so large a family rather discouraged Johanna from outward displays of maternal affection, and he could not recollect ever being caressed by her; but underneath the implacable exterior she had the interests of her children close to her heart, and on one thing she was resolved: that Richard would never follow her two husbands into the theatre.

However, with an actor for a father, it was inevitable that Wagner's strong theatrical instincts would be encouraged, by circumstance if not by design. Geyer would take along his 'little Cossack', as he called him, to rehearsals, and before long Wagner was captivated by the make-believe world of theatre. For a boy of Wagner's imaginative sensibility, the colourful scenery, the thrill of the performance and the easy fellowship of the actors, all proved irresistible and, despite Johanna's exhortations, he followed four of his brothers and sisters into a theatrical career. Geyer, who died when Wagner was eight, had always intended to make something of the boy, though his plans did not include the theatre. He would really have liked him to become a professional painter which, with

Carl Maria von Weber.

CARL MARIA VON WEBER.

the right patronage, could have been a reasonably lucrative occupation. Wagner showed no talent in this area, however, and with that obstinacy and driving sense of purpose that was to see him through the many years of disappointment ahead, he ignored the pleas of those close to him and chose the path he knew to be the right one.

Apart from introducing him to the theatre, Geyer died too young to have been able to influence significantly the boy's future development. At the age of seven, Wagner was sent to the village school at Possendorf and in September 1821 he walked the eight miles from the school back to Dresden, to be present at his stepfather's deathbed. His mother asked him to play something for Geyer on the piano in the adjoining room (Wagner's skill on the piano was at this time mainly self-taught, although he had had a few lessons at Possendorf). Following Wagner's short recital Geyer remarked, prophetically, 'Do you think he might have a talent for music?' In fact, Geyer had, unknowingly, already inspired the boy with an enthusiasm for music by introducing him

15

to his friend Carl Maria von Weber, the composer of *Der Freischütz*.

The first performance of *Der Freischütz* in June 1821 marked a turning point in the development of German music as it signified a breaking free from the domination of Italian composers such as Rossini, and the establishment of a truly German strain of Romantic opera. In Dresden, once an international centre of baroque opera, moves had been afoot for some years to establish a German national opera company, and in 1817 Weber, a young composer of the rising nationalist school, was appointed *Kapellmeister* of the court opera. In his nine years at Dresden, Weber firmly established the fame of the excellent Dresden orchestra (now known as the Staatskapelle Dresden) and captured the imagination of Germany with *Der Freischütz*.

Not least among the converts was nine-year-old Wagner, who was enraptured by the opera's supernatural horrors and the emotional intensity of the music. Weber was a frequent visitor to the household prior to Geyer's death and Wagner used to worship him as an elect being, referring to him as 'the greatest man alive'. In order to master passages from *Der Freischütz*, Wagner began to practise the piano in earnest; and indeed, he later reflected that it was Weber who first inspired him with enthusiasm for music. With Geyer's death, however, that carefree phase of rehearsals, games and make-believe came to an end and Wagner was obliged to go and live at Eisleben, Luther's home town, with Geyer's brother Karl. He returned home after a year and on 2 December 1822 entered the Dresden Kreuzschule to begin a serious education, still under the name of Richard Geyer.

3 Adolescence

Wagner spent five years at the Kreuzschule in Dresden, the beautiful rococo city on the Elbe where Napoleon had held his final court before undertaking the disastrous invasion of Russia. Dresden owed much of its magnificence to the foresight of Augustus the Strong (1670-1733), whose taste for opulent buildings and grand festivities established the court at Dresden as one of the most brilliant in Europe. In 1822 the popular Friedrich August I was still on the throne, despite being responsible for the carving up of Saxony after the Napoleonic wars. Following Napoleon's final defeat at the Battle of Waterloo in 1815, the allies met at the Congress of Vienna and punished Friedrich for his loyalty to the Emperor by annexing half his territories to Prussia. Dresden, like Leipzig, had suffered much from the ravages of war; but the stoic Protestant Saxons were determined to rebuild the fortunes of the city, and the appointment of Weber at the court opera was the first stirring of a rising German cultural awareness that was to lead to Wagner's own appointment as *Kapellmeister* to Friedrich August II in 1843.

Wagner's pupilage at the Kreuzschule provided a sobering influence on the boy's already overheated imagination, in the form of a comprehensive instruction in the classics – an important counterbalance to his rather extravagant romanticism. The study of Greek and Latin, Sophoclean tragedy, and, later, Shakespeare, served to temper his obsession with the fantastic and grotesque, as exemplified by the operas of Weber and the tales of E. T. A. Hoffmann. He did, however, develop a passion for the world of heroes, myth and legend he discovered in his reading of Greek history, particularly Homer; and it was this world that came alive in the new art form of his later music dramas.

In *Mein Leben*, Wagner's often tendentious autobiography, he was particularly generous in his praise of the school for arousing his enthusiasm for classical studies. In many ways, however, Wagner was hardly a model schoolboy. He stubbornly neglected subjects, like mathematics, that did not interest him; and although he was beginning to display some skill on the piano, he did not strike his teachers as a great achiever, either academically or musically. Indeed, by the time he left the Kreuzschule in 1827 Wagner, by then steeped in Shakespeare, was convinced his destiny lay along other paths. 'It was now beyond doubt that I was going to be a poet,' he wrote. Considering the musical heights he was to scale, this comment by the fourteen-year-old Wagner does not accord with the commonly held assumption that a genius is firmly set on the road to greatness at a very young age. Wagner, however, was certainly no infant prodigy, like Mozart who was giving public performances by the age of four. Instead, the future creator of the *Gesamtkunstwerk* – the complete work of art, a fusion of music, poetry, drama and spectacle – developed his innate gifts gradually, giving his imagination time to be influenced and moulded by the forces of change then beginning to pervade German artistic and political thought.

As a teenager, Wagner was a sensitive yet lively boy who could be at times headstrong and gregarious, at others eccentric and solitary. He always took a keen interest in what was going on around him and was quick to espouse any new intellectual fashion, whether it be musical, literary, philosophical or political. His health was so poor as a child that his mother thought he wouldn't survive, and for many years he remained pale and slim, his short body appearing too small to support his unusually large head. He suffered particularly from an allergic sensitivity of the skin (erysipelas) which troubled him throughout his lilfe, and was the main reason for the silk clothes and underwear he wore in his later years, which his enemies wrongly took to be a sign of decadence.

In spite of his physical frailty, Wagner was a mischievous youth with a great fund of vitality and derring-do, who loved climbing trees and playing with all the dogs in the neighbourhood of his house. Indeed, much of Wagner's life was spent overcoming adversity, whether it be his physical afflictions, poverty, or the hostility of those who did not understand him. As a grown man his capacity for hard work was prodigious and, as his mission to revolutionise German art became clear to him, he pursued this objective with a single-minded determination that often rode roughshod over the feelings of others, and consequently earned him many enemies along the way.

On 5 June 1826 Wagner's hero, Weber, died in London, where he had been conducting performances of his new opera, *Oberon*. Years later, in 1844, when Wagner himself was *Kapellmeister* in Dresden, he arranged, with some difficulty, to have Weber's remains transferred from London to Dresden. Wagner composed the funeral music (*Trauermusik*) for this occasion out of themes

Playbill for a London performance of *Der Freischütz*, 1826.

Adolf Wagner, Richard's uncle.

from Weber's *Euryanthe*, and after a torchlight procession he delivered a stirring oration at the graveside. According to Wagner, Weber's death turned his thoughts from heroic literature to music once again; but after his family moved to Prague in late 1826 and he went to lodge in Dresden at the house of a schoolfriend, Rudolph Böhme, he discovered that life for a boisterous pubescent boy need not be all study. He began to take an innocent interest in the attractive daughters of the household; and he and Böhme enjoyed many high-spirited adventures together, such as a marathon trek, on foot, to Prague – the first of many long journeys he undertook throughout his life.

On a school trip to Leipzig in 1827 Wagner was much taken by the carefree attitudes and colourful dress of the university students; and when his family moved back to the city later that year, he had the perfect excuse to leave Dresden abruptly and enrol in one of Leipzig's best schools, the Nikolaischule. Soon after his arrival, he renewed the acquaintance of his uncle Adolf, a scholarly, cultured disciple of Goethe, who encouraged his interest in the classics and started him on his lifelong habit of voracious reading and research. In the meantime, however, Wagner was neglecting his schoolwork to complete a huge, five-act 'Shakespearian' tragedy he had been writing for the past two years, called *Leubald*. This gory drama, full of murders, ghosts and madness, certainly horrified uncle Adolf and his mother, who saw it as an appalling waste of his time and talents.

From 1828 onwards the study of music became Wagner's

St Thomas's churchyard, Leipzig. Wagner was baptized in the Thomaskirche on the right.

19

Scene from Beethoven's *Fidelio*.

Wilhelmine Schröder-Devrient.

principal interest, and he began to take the first tentative steps towards mastering musical composition. By this time he had a new hero, Beethoven, who had died the previous March in Vienna. He had heard Beethoven's *Fidelio* overture in Dresden and been much affected by the orchestration of the piece. After hearing the Seventh Symphony at Leipzig's famous Gewandhaus, Wagner flung himself into Beethoven's music, and even thought of composing incidental music to *Leubald*, such as Beethoven had written for Goethe's *Egmont*. To help him realise this ambition, he borrowed Logier's book on composition theory from Friedrich Wieck's lending library (Wieck's daughter Clara later married Robert Schumann). However, the necessary skills did not materialise as quickly as Wagner had hoped and, as the library fines mounted, the persistent Wieck became the first of the many creditors who were to hound him throughout his life.

Not to be distracted from his purpose, Wagner began to take clandestine music lessons with a local musician, Christian Gottlieb Müller. These lessons lasted for several years and probably helped him more than the unflattering account in his autobiography suggests. Wagner's record of events in *Mein Leben* also implies that the turning point of his life occurred in Leipzig in 1829 when he heard the famous soprano Wilhelmine Schröder-Devrient sing Leonore in *Fidelio*. 'When I look back at the whole of my life,' he affirmed, 'I can discover no other experience that I could compare with this for the effect it had on me . . . she had, that evening, made me what I had sworn it was my destiny to become.' There is, however, no record of this performance taking place in Leipzig at that time; and although Wagner heard Schröder-Devrient sing Romeo in Bellini's *I Capuleti e i Montecchi* in Leipzig in 1834, a likely explanation of this probably deliberate error is that he wished it to appear that he had inherited from the outset the legacy of his spiritual predecessor, Beethoven, and brought to fruition the great German artwork that *Fidelio* had foreshadowed.

Despite the proleptic inaccuracies in *Mein Leben*, it is clear that the young Wagner was profoundly influenced by Beethoven, whose music was a revelation to him, and whose solitary life, deafness and untimely death appealed to his romantic sensibilities. Wagner's first, large-scale musical feat was to write a piano transcription of Beethoven's Choral Symphony, which he submitted (unsuccessfully) in October 1830 to Franz Schott, the publisher in Mainz. He also at this time began to make a thorough study of other Beethoven scores (as well as Mozart and Haydn symphonies), and many of his earliest compositions – mainly piano sonatas and overtures, written between 1829-31 – are influenced by Beethovenian models. Wagner was now taking his musical studies seriously (although the same could not be said of his other academic work); and, after enrolling at the Thomas-schule in Leipzig in June 1830, he started having violin lessons with Robert Sipp, a member of the Gewandhaus Orchestra. On Christmas Eve of that year, at the age of seventeen, he had an Overture in B flat major performed at a charity concert in the Leipzig Court Theatre – a less than happy occasion for the aspiring young composer, as his unusual device of inserting a *fortissimo* drumbeat in every fifth bar drew hoots of laughter from the astonished audience. Not to be deterred, in autumn 1831 Wagner began a course of lessons with Christian Theodor Weinlig, cantor of the Thomaskirche, the post held by J. S. Bach a century earlier. Weinlig realised that the boy had talent, but lacked instruction and discipline; and so he set about tempering Wagner's musical exuberance with detailed, practical exercises in harmony and counterpoint. Wagner profited greatly from his teaching and, in

Christian Theodor Weinlig.

recognition of his efforts, dedicated to Weinlig his first published work, the Piano Sonata in B flat major.

Nobody was more delighted with Wagner's progress in his lessons with Weinlig than his mother, who was becoming increasingly despairing of her son's dissolute ways. After entering the Thomas-schule and, later, Leipzig University, all serious study (apart from musical activities) went by the wayside, as he gave himself up to a life of dissipation. He joined the rowdy student societies, frequented the gambling dens and taverns, and at one point was faced with the prospect of several duels – none of which, luckily for him, ever took place.

In the autumn of 1830 Wagner found himself, not for the last time in his life, caught up in a revolution. The effects of the July Revolution in Paris – three days of rioting in which bourgeoisie and workers alike rebelled against the reactionary Charles X and established Louis Philippe on the throne of France – had spread to Leipzig, where there was resentment against growing corruption amongst city officials, and against the ineffectual Catholic royal house of Saxony. In a night of noisy unrest, Wagner joined the mob of students who drank and sang in the streets, ransacked a brothel and marched to the prison to demonstrate to the authorities their youthful indignation. Later, when the working classes (who had a genuine grievance) rose up in defiance and started to threaten property, the students were commissioned by the same authorities to arm themselves and protect the factories of the wealthy entrepreneurs against the rabble – a task they (including Wagner) undertook with some zeal, clearly oblivious to the ironies of the situation.

In 1832 Wagner's formal musical education came to an end. He had what he considered to be a reasonable *oeuvre* of works to his name, some of which had been performed in his native city; and as he had just completed his most ambitious project to date – the Symphony in C major – he decided it was time to seek recognition further afield. Armed with several of his compositions, Wagner made the journey to Vienna, which was at that time falling under the spell of the dance music of the Strauss family. Disillusioned by the prevailing artistic climate there, Wagner left Vienna for Bohemia, which had always held a romantic attraction for him – especially so since his memorable journey to Prague in 1827, when he had made the acquaintance of a friend of his sister, named Jenny, one of the beautiful, aristocratic daughters of Count Pachta. It was to his estate that Wagner headed in late 1832 and where, in the throes of tortured passion, he began to compose *Die Hochzeit*, his first attempt at a full-scale opera.

4 Early Operas

While staying at Count Pachta's estate, Wagner fell in love for the first time, with Jenny, the taller and darker of the Count's two nubile daughters. From what he told his friend Theodor Apel, his youthful infatuation knew no bounds, seeing in Jenny 'an ideal of beauty' who represented everything his heart desired. His love, however, was not requited and he felt the disappointment all the more keenly because his infatuation had blinded him to the realities of the situation. Being well-born, the girls would have expected to marry into a similar social class (which disqualified Wagner from the start), and Jenny probably never considered him as a serious contender for her hand. To tease Wagner, the girls both used to flirt shamelessly with the coarse, horsey, upper-class cavaliers who were in constant attendance, and who Wagner hated. Eventually he lost his patience with Jenny's amorous games and, exasperated, he berated her for her shallow tastes and frivolous lifestyle. After much moonlight agonising in the grounds of the Count's castle, Wagner decided that the fair Jenny was not worthy of his love and, with heavy heart, he left Prague for Leipzig in December 1832, armed with the text of *Die Hochzeit* (The Wedding), a lurid monument to unfulfilled passion.

Silhouette of Wagner, 1835.

In Leipzig, Wagner composed a septet and the music for the first scene (which has survived) of *Die Hochzeit*, both of which won the approval of his old master, Weinlig. However, his favourite sister Rosalie, an actress with good connections in Leipzig, disliked the text and, in deference to her judgement, Wagner destroyed the manuscript, probably realising that the work would have had little chance of ever being staged. As well as writing the libretto of *Die Hochzeit*, during his short stay in Prague Wagner heard his Symphony in C major, his last exercise in late classical instrumental music, performed by the students of the Prague Conservatory – a small triumph for the young composer which must have provided some consolation for his unlucky experience in love. The symphony received two further performances shortly

Heinrich Laube.

afterwards in Leipzig, where it was warmly praised by public and critics alike. At the second of these performances, in January 1833, the symphony was given a good notice by Heinrich Laube, the editor of *Die Zeitung für die elegante Welt*, the organ of a radical youth movement of the 1830s known as *Das junge Deutschland* (Young Germany). Laube, a friend of Wagner's sister Rosalie, was the intellectual leader of this literary movement, which attacked the social, moral and political conditions of the time, and advocated a German art free from academic and classical constraints. Wagner was much taken by Laube's sincerity, bluntness and sense of justice, and his influence found its way into his early writings and stage works.

Impressed by Wagner's symphony, Laube offered him the libretto of an opera he had just written, which he had intended to send to Meyerbeer, the popular German composer who was to assist Wagner on several occasions in the years ahead. Flattered as Wagner must have been by the offer, he had already decided that he would only write music to his own words; and indeed, at no time in his life did he ever seriously contemplate using another

24

librettist. By this time, he had begun work on the text of his first complete opera, *Die Feen* (The Fairies), based on Carlo Gozzi's play *La donna serpente*. This coincided with his acceptance of an offer from his brother Albert to take a job as chorus master at the theatre in Würzburg, where Albert was on the musical staff. In February 1833, a month after taking up his new post, Wagner completed the libretto of *Die Feen*, and composed the entire musical score by January the following year.

Die Feen was very much a product of the prevailing fashion in Germany at that time for the supernatural and the fantastic, a vogue established by the operas of Weber and the tales of E. T. A. Hoffmann. The plot, which contains certain dramatic themes developed in Wagner's later operas (such as the forbidden question and redemption through love), concerns the love of a mortal prince, Arindal, for a fairy called Ada, who agrees to marry him on condition he doesn't ask who she is. His curiosity gets the better of him and they are forced to part. Ada wishes to join him as his earthly wife, but can only do this if he promises never to waver in his loyalty to her, however strong the temptation. So terrible are the tests she puts him through, however, that he eventually curses her and she is turned into stone. Tormented with grief, he follows her into the underworld and restores her to life by the magic of his lyre. As a reward, he is allowed to stay with Ada in fairyland for ever after.

In his first opera Wagner was content to test his blossoming talent within the framework of conventional opera forms. The traditional recitative, aria, duet and chorus are still very much in evidence (as indeed they are, though to a lesser and lesser degree, in every opera until *Das Rheingold*, his first true 'music drama') but, like the story, the music of *Die Feen* contains echoes of Wagner's more mature style, especially in its skilfully crafted ensemble passages, its often bold dissonances and use of simple recurring *motifs*.

At Würzburg, while composing *Die Feen*, Wagner was expected to earn his keep, and he soon came to realise that great artistry was rarely the order of the day at a small, under-funded provincial theatre. One of his first jobs was to train the chorus for their parts in Heinrich Marschner's *Der Vampyr*, for which he composed a florid concluding allegro for Aubry's aria, sung by his brother Albert. During his year in Würzburg he learned a lot about the practicalities of running an opera house and familiarised himself with the work of many different composers. He also experienced what he referred to as his first love affair, with Therese Ringelmann, one of the chorus sopranos, which stopped well short of the altar but gave him a taste for romantic interludes that he was eagerly to cultivate on more than one occasion.

25

In January 1834 Wagner returned to Leipzig with the finished score of *Die Feen*, convinced that his new opera would be a success. However, Franz Hauser, manager of the Leipzig theatre, thought differently (despite the fact that Wagner's sister Rosalie had put in a good word for him) and, to Wagner's horror, rejected the opera. In fact, *Die Feen* did not receive its first performance until June 1888 in Munich, five years after his death. Wagner's disappointment was soon overshadowed by another artistic experience that led him to question his preconceptions on the merits of German versus Italian opera. Wilhelmine Schröder-Devrient was in Leipzig singing Romeo in Bellini's *I Capuleti e i Montecchi* and, after hearing her performance, Wagner was drawn to pay homage to the vocal beauty of Italian opera in his first published essay, *Die deutsche Oper* (German Opera), which appeared in *Die Zeitung für die elegante Welt* in June 1834. In it he criticised the academic tendencies of German composers such as Spohr, Marschner, and even Weber, in favour of Bellini, who knew how to write music full of warmth, expressiveness, and passion. Bellini became one of Wagner's heroes and for the rest of his life he retained a sense of gratitude to the Italian for opening his eyes to the emotional power of simple song.

While under the spell of Bellini's music, Wagner took a holiday with his friend Theodor Apel at Teplitz, in Bohemia, where he wrote the first outline of his new opera *Das Liebesverbot* (The Ban on Love), based loosely on Shakespeare's *Measure for Measure*, which was to be his tribute to Italian spontaneity and sensuality. (Later in life he dismissed this sparkling opera as the 'wild' work of his youth, finding little of value in it.) Upon returning from Bohemia, Wagner discovered that he had been offered a job as music director of Heinrich Bethmann's theatre troupe, based in Magdeburg, but in July 1834 doing a summer season in Bad Lauchstadt. Within a week of joining this rather disreputable troupe of players, he made his début as an opera conductor with Mozart's *Don Giovanni* which, despite lack of rehearsal, went off to everybody's satisfaction. While staying in lodgings in Lauchstadt, Wagner met and soon fell in love with the actress Minna Planer, an attractive girl with dark hair and blue eyes who was nearly four years his senior. Her distinctive appearance had ensured her success on the stage and, inevitably, had given rise to many amorous advances by theatre managers and well-to-do patrons – advances that she did not always feel it was in the interests of her career to resist.

Minna had been seduced at the age of fifteen by an army officer, Ernst Rudolf von Einsiedel, and left with a child, Natalie, who was brought up as her sister. Perhaps because of this bitter experience, Minna did not show a capacity for deep and passionate

Bellini.

love, but she clearly held the key to a fundamental need in Wagner to possess some aspect of the feminine principle, whether sexual or maternal, or both. This question of what Wagner saw in a woman who neither understood him nor had faith in his genius is made no clearer by Wagner's own account in *Mein Leben*. His comment that he was attracted only by Minna's 'agreeable and fresh appearance' was possibly said in the interests of diplomacy, as Wagner's second wife, Cosima, wrote *Mein Leben* at his dictation. It does not accord with letters he wrote to Minna and Theodor Apel at the time, which show that he was deeply in love and terrified at the thought of losing her.

When the troupe moved to Magdeburg in late 1834, Wagner and Minna went with them, and for the next year Wagner kept busy with his conducting duties and the composition of *Das Liebesverbot*. The musical highlight of this period was in April 1835, when Schröder-Devrient came to Magdeburg for a series of performances under Wagner, which further enhanced his reputation as a highly proficient conductor. The company, however, was on the point of bankruptcy and was disbanded soon after the Magdeburg première of *Das Liebesverbot* on 29 March 1836. Wagner proceeded to Berlin in a fruitless attempt to get his opera staged at the Königstadt theatre; and then on to Königsberg in pursuit of Minna, who had accepted a theatre engagement there, hoping that Wagner could do likewise. On 24 November 1836 Wagner and Minna were married in the church in Tragheim, near Königsberg, a hastily decided and ill-considered match that was soon to lead to recriminations and resentment from both sides. Right from the start, the marriage was dogged by insecurity and money problems. Wagner was not appointed to the musical directorship of the Königsberg theatre until April 1837, by which time he had amassed considerable debts that he had no way of repaying.

As it turned out, the theatre was also on the verge of bankruptcy and could not even pay Wagner his salary. This was the last straw for Minna who, already tired of the hand-to-mouth existence and the violent arguments, secretly departed for Dresden at the end of

Minna Planer, Wagner's first wife.

May with a businessman called Dietrich. Wagner chased after her in a jealous rage and, after the usual tears and reproaches, she agreed to return to him if he could get a secure job. As luck would have it, in June 1837 he was offered the post of music director at the theatre in Riga, a historic Baltic port in Latvia with a large German community. Wagner arrived there in August, confident that a change of scenery would spur his creativity (the past year had been a time of low productivity) and save his marriage. Wagner and Minna were finally reunited in October, after Minna had written to him apologising for her conduct and asking for his forgiveness. Headstrong as ever, Wagner began to make waves in Riga with an ambitious programme of concerts and proposals for sweeping theatrical reforms – activities that did not endear him to the director of the Riga theatre, Karl von Holtei, whom he soon came to regard as his worst enemy.

During his time in Riga, Wagner worked on the libretto and music of a new grand opera, the subject of which he had decided upon after reading Edward Bulwer Lytton's novel *Rienzi, the Last of the Roman Tribunes* in the summer of 1837. Holtei had to leave Riga suddenly in January 1839 to avoid embarrassing disclosures about his personal life and, as a parting shot, appointed Wagner's friend Heinrich Dorn as conductor for the coming season. Finding himself once again out of a job, and with his creditors at his heels, Wagner planned a secret escape across the Russian border (Riga was then part of the Russian Empire) into East Prussia. His chosen destination was Paris, where he hoped to find fame and fortune and acceptance for his new opera, far from the petty confines of German provincial theatre.

5 Paris

Minna Planer.

Wagner knew that his escape from Riga could not be accomplished in a conventional fashion for, as debtors, both his and his wife's passports had been confiscated by the authorities. Therefore, with the help of an old friend, Abraham Möller, Wagner planned an illicit crossing of the Russian frontier – a dangerous course of action, particularly as it was patrolled by armed Cossacks trained to shoot fugitives on sight. After spending an evening at a smuggler's den, Wagner, Minna and their Newfoundland dog Robber scrambled across the frontier ditch and made a dash into Prussian territory, luckily unseen by the patrolling sentries. There they made their way to the port of Pillau in a rickety cart, which at one point overturned in a farmyard, causing some injury to Minna. At Pillau, the Wagners and their dog boarded the *Thetis*, a small schooner with a crew of seven, bound for London. After a week's sailing, a violent storm forced them to take shelter in a Norwegian fjord, going ashore at a small fishing village called Sandwike. Wagner later claimed in *Mein Leben* that the sound of the sailors' shouts echoing around the granite walls of the fjord gave him the inspiration for the seamen's song in *Der fliegende Holländer* (The Flying Dutchman), which was 'already present in my mind, and now acquired a distinct poetic and musical colour'.

After enduring more storms, the *Thetis* finally arrived in England in August 1839, where the exhausted Wagners disembarked and made their way to London. There, Wagner looked up Sir George Smart, conductor of the Philharmonic Society, to whom he had earlier sent the score of his flamboyant *Rule Britannia* overture; but Sir George was out of town. Wagner had no more luck in locating Bulwer Lytton, the author of *Rienzi*; and, after a few days' sightseeing, he and Minna left for France, arriving in Boulogne by Channel steamer, where they remained for nearly a month. By coincidence, Meyerbeer, then the darling of the Paris Opéra, was staying in Boulogne at that time and

30

Wagner decided to pay his respects to the esteemed composer of *Robert le Diable* and *Les Huguenots*– works which greatly appealed to the French bourgeoisie's taste for simple, showy spectacle.

Although Wagner came to despise Meyerbeer and everything he stood for, in 1839 his feelings towards him were ambivalent. He was convinced of the essential transparency of Meyerbeer's operas, yet he was impressed by his undeniable success and felt that German composers could learn a lot from Meyerbeer's achievements in the development of dramatic music. At their first meeting in Boulogne, Meyerbeer received him kindly and listened patiently as Wagner read him the first three acts of the *Rienzi* libretto, and agreed to study the (only just completed) orchestral score of the first two acts. On a subsequent visit he gave Wagner a letter of recommendation to Charles Duponchel, director of the Paris Opéra. Armed with this piece of good fortune, Wagner and Minna left Boulogne for Paris, arriving there on 17 September 1839.

Wagner's first Paris sojurn was a time of unmitigated poverty and disappointment, which was to have a profound impact on the future development of his art. He always recalled with bitterness these two-and-a-half years in which he failed to make his name as a composer, and took the opportunity in *Mein Leben* to launch scathing attacks on those he felt responsible for his misfortune – especially the hapless Meyerbeer, who came to be on the receiving end of some of Wagner's most libellous prose. Wagner and Minna

Sir George Smart.

arrived in the Paris of Louis Philippe at a time when the bourgeois élite had attained a position of enormous wealth and power. In a society where money could guarantee limitless indulgence, musical tastes were similarly biased towards extravagance on a grand scale. Magnificent settings, endless ballets and noisy choruses were the order of the day, and the Paris Opéra, by then the epitome of vulgar luxury, more than fulfilled these requirements.

In Paris, Wagner soon discovered that without money and connnections, letters of recommendation (even from so illustrious a composer as Meyerbeer) alone carried little weight with the world-weary management of the Opéra. Duponchel politely dismissed him as another young hopeful and Wagner never heard from him again. Desperate to make himself known – and to earn some money – Wagner resorted to composing songs and occasional pieces for famous singers, but this expediency failed to produce any results. Parisian society, as Wagner came to realise with growing indignation, was totally unresponsive to anything that was not gaudily dressed or ostentatiously presented. Unlike Liszt and Chopin, who were at the height of their fame and the rage of Parisian salon society, Wagner lacked the attributes needed for entry to fashionable circles. He was not a virtuoso on the piano or violin, his manners and appearance were those of an unrefined, provincial German, and his only friends were a few of his fellow countrymen as poor and lacking in influence as himself.

In March 1840, however, Wagner's luck seemed about to change when the Théâtre de la Renaissance, at Meyerbeer's

Meyerbeer.

Chopin.

prompting, provisionally agreed to put on a performance of *Das Liebesverbot*. Unfortunately, the next month the theatre went bankrupt and was forced to close – an outcome that Wagner later claimed in *Mein Leben* was foreseen by Meyerbeer, who for reasons of his own had deliberately deceived him. This claim should perhaps be seen in the light of other unflattering references to Meyerbeer in *Mein Leben*, which never acknowledge the help he gave Wagner on more than one occasion in Paris – help that Wagner was always more than ready to accept. Driven to desperation by the closure of the Théâtre de la Renaissance, Wagner took the initiative and obtained work from publisher Maurice Schlesinger arranging other composers' music, which brought in some much-needed cash while he worked on the orchestral score of *Rienzi*. In fact, this work, together with reviews and essays he wrote for various journals, was more extensive than had previously been realised and by the time Wagner left Paris it had amassed into a considerable body of work.

Despite the tribulations he had to endure in Paris, Wagner's small circle of friends – which included the German painter Friedrich Pecht – attest to his unfailing resilience, his sharp humour and his love of company. In 1839, Wagner's old Leipzig friend, Heinrich Laube, visited Paris with his new wife and introduced him to the writer Heinrich Heine, whose work Wagner much admired. Wagner apparently took delight in recounting to the little group the story of his recent adventures at sea, which even the icy Heine found hugely amusing. After a year in Paris, Wagner's friends noted a growing maturity in him that expressed itself in deepening artistic convictions. Wagner himself claimed that this change in his life could be credited to one specific event: his rediscovery of Beethoven's Ninth Symphony in a rehearsal by the Paris Conservatoire orchestra which, according to *Mein Leben*, opened his eyes afresh to the beauty of the music and the glories of

Rienzi, finale of Act II.

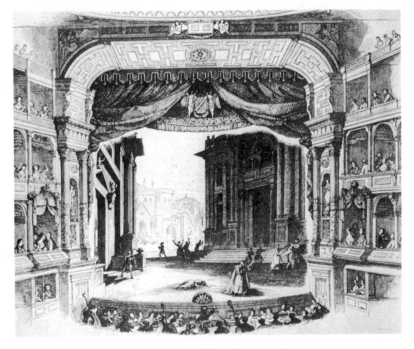

German art. His new enthusiasm found literary expression in a
short story, *A Pilgrimage to Beethoven*, in which he outlined his
future task to combine symphony and song in the music drama.
Wagner also claimed in *Mein Leben* that this performance of the
Ninth Symphony inspired him to compose a 'German' work, the
Faust Overture in D minor, which he completed on 12 January
1840. However, there is good reason to suppose that this work was
influenced not by Beethoven's Ninth, but by Berlioz's dramatic
symphony *Roméo et Juliette*, one of the first performances of which
Wagner attended at the end of 1839. Wagner was greatly
impressed by the orchestration of the symphony, which he admits
to studying in great detail; and his criticism of Berlioz in *Mein
Leben*, together with his version of the genesis of the *Faust*
Overture, could be intended to promote Beethoven to a position of
central importance in the development of Wagnerian music
drama, while playing down the influence of the French composer.

Wagner completed the final score of *Rienzi* in November 1840,
at a time when his financial position was getting steadily worse. In
fact, in a letter to Theodor Apel in October, Minna claimed he had
been forced to work on the opera from a debtors' prison – though
(typically) this may have been a ploy to extract money from Apel.
Right from its conception, Wagner regarded *Rienzi* as a 'grand
opera' in the French and Italian style, with all its associated scenic
and musical splendour; and he set out to 'outdo all previous
examples with sumptuous extravagance'. As a particularly noisy
example of mid-nineteenth century grand opera, the five-act

Scene from *Der fliegende Holländer*.

Rienzi achieved considerable popularity in Wagner's lifetime; though Wagner himself soon turned against the opera, referring to it as early as 1845 as a 'monster'. *Rienzi* does, however, contain some memorable passages, such as the swelling A on the trumpets at the beginning of the overture, and the 'Santo Spirito, Cavalieri' melody; but at other times the strong influence of Meyerbeer and Spontini is more than obvious, and it is a pointless exercise to try to place the opera in the tradition of true Wagnerian music drama. With Meyerbeer's help, Wagner succeeded in having the work accepted, in June 1841, for performance at the Royal Court Theatre in Dresden. The première, on 20 October 1842, lasted six hours and was an overwhelming success.

While completing *Rienzi*, Wagner was also working on the prose sketch of *Der fliegende Holländer*, the idea for which, he claimed in *Mein Leben*, had been ever-present in his mind since the *Thetis* voyage. In May 1840 Wagner sent Meyerbeer's principal librettist Eugène Scribe the prose draft of the new opera with a view to collaborating with Scribe on a libretto. The next month he sent the draft to Meyerbeer himself, hoping that he would bring it to the attention of the new director of the Opéra, Léon Pillet. Wagner hoped to receive a commission from the Opéra to write the music, and for the purposes of an audition he composed the text and music of three numbers – Senta's Ballad, and the choruses of the Norwegian sailors and the Dutchman's crew. Pillet apparently liked the story, but didn't want Wagner to write the music, and told him that it would be at least seven years

36

before he could be offered even the smallest commission. However, Pillet offered to buy the prose draft for 500 francs, so that he could have it made into an opera by one of the composers under contract to him. Wagner prudently accepted this offer in July 1841, as by this time work on his own composition of *Der fliegende Holländer* was well under way. The draft was handed to two librettists who availed themselves of the Flying Dutchman legend to write *Le Vaisseau Fantôme*, which was set to music by Pierre-Louis Dietsch and performed at the Paris Opéra in November 1842 – ironically the same month that rehearsals for *Der fliegende Holländer* began in Dresden.

Wagner completed the musical composition of *Der fliegende Holländer* in the summer of 1841 and in November sent the full score to Count Wilhelm von Redern, intendant of the Berlin Court Opera. At the same time, Wagner once again appealed to Meyerbeer for help; and following his generous recommendation, Redern accepted the opera for performance. (In the end, the première took place in Dresden on 2 January 1843.) Although some of Wagner's recollections regarding the genesis of *Der*

Scene from *Der fliegende Holländer*.

fliegende Holländer may be inaccurate, it is safe to assume that the main literary source for the opera was Heinrich Heine's *Memoirs of Herr von Schnabelewopski* (1834), in which a Dutch captain, who rashly swears 'by all the devils in hell' to round a certain Cape, is doomed by the Devil to sail the seas until the Last Judgement, unless he is redeemed by the fidelity of a woman's love. Wagner's Dutchman, allowed to come ashore every seven years to seek redemption (a central and recurring theme in Wagner's operas), is rescued from his plight by Senta who, filled with pity and a deep sense of destiny, forsakes her lover Erik and assures the Dutchman that she will be true to him unto death. At the end, in an ultimate act of sacrifice, she hurls herself over a cliff into the sea, so ensuring the Dutchman's salvation.

In *A Communication to my Friends* (1851), Wagner states that by composing Senta's second act Ballad in May-June 1840, before the rest of the opera, he 'unwittingly planted the thematic seed of all the music in the opera', which 'quite involuntarily spread out over the entire drama in a complete, unbroken web'. Again, this retrospective interpretation of events suggests a maturity of vision in the young composer that is by no means substantiated by the evidence, in this case the score of *Der fliegende Holländer*. Although the opera is a radical departure from his earlier works – especially in the growing use of *motifs* and through-composed scenes – it still contains many of the trappings of conventional opera, such as arias and duets; and in terms of structural organisation, is still a long way from the motivic and harmonic complexities of *Das Rheingold*. However, *Der fliegende Holländer* is

Illustration showing three costume designs (Dutchman, Senta and Erik) from the première of *Der fliegende Holländer*.

38

Final scene of *Der fliegende Holländer*, as Senta throws herself off the cliff.

far enough down the road towards music drama to justify Wagner's assertion that this opera marked the beginning of his career as a poet, as opposed to a mere manufacturer of librettos.

During the winter of 1841-2, Wagner's thoughts turned to Germany once again, his nostalgia fuelled by his reading of German sagas and Friedrich Raumer's *History of the Hohenstaufen*. This book inspired him to write a prose sketch for an opera in five acts called *Die Sarazenin* (The Saracen Woman), which was immediately cast to one side when he came across another legend of the German Middle Ages, that of Tannhäuser and Venus, which he realised had far greater dramatic potential. Deeply disillusioned with Paris, Wagner now looked to Germany to provide the right climate for the revolution in musical taste which he hoped to bring about. Now that *Rienzi* and *Der fliegende Holländer* had both been accepted for performance, he was anxious to return to his homeland and, after bidding a tearful farewell to his faithful friends, he and Minna left the boulevards of Paris and began the long journey back to Dresden.

6 Royal Kapellmeister

Original designs for
Tannhäuser.

As Wagner and Minna passed through the Rhineland, the weather
was cold and grey, in stark contrast to the bright spring sunshine
they had left behind in Paris. After the degradations he had
suffered during the last two-and-a-half years, the return to his
homeland was an uplifting experience for Wagner. 'As I beheld
the Rhine for the first time,' he wrote in the *Autobiographical
Sketch* (1843), 'my eyes filled with tears, and I swore that I would,
although only a poor artist, devote my life to my German
fatherland.' Driving along the valley of the Wartburg, outside
Eisenach, the weather suddenly improved and a few rays of
sunshine illuminated the legendary castle high in the mountains,
where in the thirteenth century the courtly *Minnesänger* had held
song contests, in which the knights would compose verses on the
nature of love. Wagner's patriotism (which had a cultural rather
than political bias at this time) had been fuelled by his reading of
German medieval legend in Paris and this view of the Wartburg
turned his thoughts once again to the Tannhäuser legend. Indeed,
the scene remained so vividly in his mind that he was able, three
years later, to describe it in detail to the Parisian stage designer
who painted the sets for the Dresden première of his next opera,
Tannhäuser.

Wagner and Minna arrived back in Dresden on 12 April 1842
and it was not long before his new-found enthusiasm for Germany
turned to disillusionment. The city in which he had spent much of
his childhood 'seemed cold and dead in the wild, gloomy weather'.
He was delighted to see his mother and the other members of the
family again after six years' absence, but many of his old friends
had since disappeared; and, equally upsetting, the stuffy officials
of the Dresden opera made it quite clear that they found him all
too excitable and impatient. The only exceptions were Wilhelm
Fischer, the stage manager and chorus master, and Ferdinand
Heine, the costume designer, both of whom took a strong liking to
Wagner and did all they could to help him during the rehearsals of

Rienzi. In spite of these new friendships, however, Wagner soon decided that in just about every respect the Dresden he had once known and loved had vanished. It now seemed a hostile place, and, in a letter to his Paris friend Samuel Lehrs, he reflected that if he was going to be a failure he would rather it be in Paris than in Dresden:

I have no geographical preferences and my homeland, apart from its beautiful ranges of hills, woods and valleys, actually repels me. These Saxons are an accursed bunch – mean, slow, oafish, idle and coarse – why should I have anything to do with them?

Within a week of arriving back in Germany, Wagner made his way

Mendelssohn.

41

Herman Winckelman in the title role, *Tannhäuser*.

to Berlin to discuss the staging of *Der fliegende Holländer* with the intendant of the Court Opera, Count Redern, who had accepted the score on Meyerbeer's recommendation while Wagner was still in Paris. In Berlin, Wagner learned that Redern was about to retire and was to be succeeded by Theodor Küstner, who, having already rejected the opera in Munich, was decidedly less enthusiastic about the project. Küstner could not very well turn down outright a work which had already been accepted by his predecessor, but instead he procrastinated long enough to delay the Berlin performance of *Der fliegende Holländer* until 7 January 1844, a year after its eventual première in Dresden. After this disappointment, Wagner turned against Berlin, with its 'pretensions to greatness', although he was prudent enough to recognise that a success in Berlin would represent an enormous boost to his career. He continued to set high hopes on the patronage of the King of Prussia, Friedrich Wilhelm IV, who wished to establish the city as the cultural capital of Germany. Both Meyerbeer and Mendelssohn held official posts in Berlin at the time, but even Meyerbeer's influence had failed to secure a performance of the *Holländer*, and Wagner's appeals to Mendelssohn for help fell on deaf ears. The privations Wagner suffered while trying to establish himself in Paris and Berlin made him all the more bitter towards these and other Jewish composers, whose popularity he felt barred the way to the acceptance of his own unique genius. He deeply resented the success of what he saw as second-rate music, written just for entertainment and financial gain. This resentment, tinged with envy, led him to make virulent attacks on Meyerbeer and later to engage in scurrilous theorising in which he blamed the Jews for all that was wrong in contemporary music.

In June 1842, before the *Rienzi* rehearsals began in earnest, Wagner took a holiday with Minna and his mother in Teplitz, the spa he had visited with his friend Theodor Apel in 1834. While there, Wagner took off by himself for a few days' ramble in the Bohemian mountains where, inspired by the idyllic scenery, he sketched out the three-act plan of *Tannhäuser*. In July, Wagner cut short his holiday and returned to Dresden to take charge of the impending rehearsals, which were due to take place under the *Kapellmeister*, Karl Gottlieb Reissiger. The cast, which included Schröder-Devrient and the *Heldentenor* Joseph Tichatschek, greatly enjoyed rehearsing the opera, and Wagner's presence there increased their enthusiasm. Tichatschek, who was singing Rienzi, the Roman tribune, was so taken with the B minor ensemble in the Act III finale that he proposed every member of the cast should pay Wagner a silver penny each time it was rehearsed – a ritual that was duly carried out, to Wagner's delight. 'None of them

Scene from the Venusberg in *Tannhäuser*.

suspected,' he confessed, 'that this money they gave me as a joke, actually helped to pay for our daily food.'

The première took place on 20 October and was a huge success, with Wagner being hauled onto the stage after each act to receive the tumultuous applause. As pleased as anybody was the management of the opera house, who realised they had a money-earner on their hands, which they could put on again and again without having to pay Wagner a penny more than the flat fee of 300 thalers. (This arrangement was quite normal: except for Berlin, no German opera house paid royalties.) The public realised that *Rienzi* represented something new and audacious in grand opera, and the story – in which Rienzi ends the corrupt rule of the aristocracy and is made tribune of the people – probably captured the imaginations of the German middle classes, who were becoming increasingly discontented with their princely rulers and feared that, since the Congress of Vienna in 1815, Germany was sliding into a new age of feudalism.

The première of *Der fliegende Holländer* followed shortly afterwards, on 2 January 1843, and was a qualified success. The public warmed to Schröder-Devrient's performance as Senta, though after the colourful extravagance of *Rienzi*, they were rather taken aback by the brooding, gloomy quality of *Der fliegende*

Holländer; and Wagner had the first intimations that audiences and professional musicians alike would not always be in tune with his inner visions. A few days after this première, Wagner received an offer from Freiherr von Lüttichau, intendant of the Dresden Court Theatre, of an assistant conductor's post which had become vacant; but Wagner, realising that it would be difficult in this subordinate post to enforce all the administrative changes that he felt necessary, turned down the offer on the grounds that he 'would need authority in the full sense of the word'. He also feared that the post would conflict with his own composing, at a time when his productive powers were 'at their most vigorous'. Lüttichau persisted, offering him the post on a permanent basis for a salary of 1500 thalers a year. For a man in Wagner's financial position, with a wife who was eager for middle-class security and respectability, it was too good an offer to turn down and his appointment as *Kapellmeister* to the court of the King of Saxony was announced on 2 February 1843.

Gluck.

44

Letter from Wagner asking to borrow 1,000 Thalers for an imminent project.

As *Kapellmeister*, Wagner was responsible for all the musical activities of the court, including conducting opera and orchestral concerts and composing pieces for special court occasions. In Germany much value was placed on these appointments, which were tenable for life and had a kudos value which more than compensated for the modest financial remuneration. The *Kapellmeister* was very much a court servant, however, and as such was expected to look and act the part. Wagner was obliged to have a court uniform made, costing 100 thalers, an outgoing he regarded as 'ridiculous'. This private expression of dissent was the start of a long, stormy and all too public campaign against the musical and political establishment of the Dresden court, that was to end with Wagner's exile from Germany. In particular, his originality as a conductor aggravated some of the singers and members of the orchestra, although his novel readings of some of the classics usually carried the day with the public. The King, Friedrich August II, had a great liking for Gluck's operas, and Wagner scored an early success with a performance of *Armide*. He followed this up, to similar acclaim, with the same composer's *Iphigenia in Aulis*, which he revised and conducted in February 1847.

Wagner completed the text of *Tannhäuser* in the spring of 1843, though an excess of feverish excitement prevented him from beginning the composition sketch until November, and the full score was not completed until 13 April 1845. While working on *Tannhäuser*, Wagner threw himself enthusiastically into his new role of Royal *Kapellmeister*. Suddenly in possession of a moderate amount of money, he and Minna moved into a spacious new apartment, complete with a new concert grand piano, and he settled in comfortably to his lifelong habit of spending beyond his means. In particular, he continued to build up his vast library, which contained a carefully chosen range of ancient and modern literature from which he drew the subject matter of his later music dramas. A few weeks after his appointment, Wagner told his friend Samuel Lehrs that 'I have been told quite bluntly that I am expected to reorganise musical affairs here, along genuinely artistic lines.'

Unfortunately, Wagner's own interpretation of his brief was soon to bring him into direct conflict with many of the more hidebound factions in Dresden's musical establishment, not least of whom were members of the Dresden Orchestra. Three weeks after his initial success with Gluck's *Armide*, Wagner conducted a controversial performance of Mozart's *Don Giovanni*, during the rehearsals for which he clashed endlessly with the orchestra over tempos, and began an ongoing slanging match with its vociferous leader, Karl Lipinski, who complained to the board of

45

management about Wagner's treatment of this hallowed classic. Indeed, his fresh approach to the operas of Mozart, whom he revered, was used as ammunition to discredit him by the anti-Wagner faction throughout his time in Dresden.

One of Wagner's duties as *Kapellmeister* was to write music for special occasions and in the summer of 1844 he composed 'A Salute to Friedrich August the Beloved from his Loyal Subjects', a choral work for male voices which foreshadowed the famous march from *Tannhäuser*. That July he conducted the first performance of *Das Liebesmahl der Apostel* (The Love-Feast of the Apostles), a work for men's voices written for a huge choral festival he had helped organise, which drew singers from all over Saxony to the Frauenkirche in Dresden. Wagner's biblical scene was performed by a mighty 1200 strong choir, divided into separate choruses of disciples and apostles and accompanied by an orchestra of 100 players. Apart from musical duties, the post of Royal *Kapellmeister* gave Wagner the opportunity to get involved in political events connected with the Court Opera, and in the autumn of 1844 he was elected to a committee which had been trying in vain for some time to arrange for the transfer of Weber's remains from London to Dresden. With Wagner's help, the obstacles were at last overcome and, on 14 December 1844, Weber's coffin was taken in procession from the banks of the Elbe to the Catholic cemetery, a highly moving occasion for which Wagner composed the *Trauermusik* for wind instruments and delivered a heartfelt address at the graveside.

In spite of the success of *Rienzi* and *Der fliegende Holländer* in Dresden, Wagner's financial situation continued to worsen. With creditors continually at his heels, some of them going back even to his schooldays, his only recourse was to pay off old debts by incurring new ones, usually by borrowing from his friends, whom he believed were duty-bound to help him out in his hour of need. 'They must not look on me as someone who needs help on his own account, but as an artist and a movement in art which they want to preserve for the future and not allow to founder,' he wrote to Ferdinand Heine in 1849.

An obvious source of income for Wagner was his operas and so, after the first few performances of *Rienzi* and *Der fliegende Holländer*, he looked around for a publisher. Breitkopf & Härtel expressed interest in the scores, but were not prepared to offer him a fee. After further fruitless wrangling, Wagner therefore took the fateful decision to publish the scores himself. The court publisher C. F. Meser agreed to print them on a 10 per cent commission basis and Wagner obtained the necessary capital from three loyal friends. Unfortunately, every one of the theatres around Germany to which Wagner sent copies of the scores returned them, so foiling Wagner's hopes of achieving success outside Dresden, and leaving him in such financial straits that he was forced to ask for an advance of 5000 thalers from the court orchestra pension fund. As well as the lack of demand for the scores, Meser's business acumen left a lot to be desired. Even when demand for Wagner's music picked up after 1850, Meser threw away a lot of opportunities by being over-cautious. 'Of all the music publishers in the world he is the least fit for such a business,' Wagner wrote to his friend Theodor Uhlig in 1851. 'If you distilled the quintessence of the most terrified, unreliable and cowardly philistine, what you would get is Meser.'

After finishing the score of *Tannhäuser* in April 1845, Wagner resolved to spend a year of study in his library before embarking on a new opera, not realising that the creative process had already started. In July 1845, Wagner and Minna went on a holiday to Marienbad in Bohemia to 'take the cure' (Wagner suffered from skin troubles and gastric disorders throughout his life). Every morning he went walking in the woods with Wolfram von Eschenbach's *Titurel* and *Parzifal*, and the old epic poem of *Lohengrin* which he had already encountered in Paris. His re-reading of the legend of Lohengrin, the Knight of the Grail, fired his imagination, and soon began to take dramatic shape in his

Act II, Scene 4 of *Tannhäuser*.

47

mind. Under doctor's orders to avoid any form of excitement, Wagner sought some light relief in drafting a comedy based around the old Mastersingers' guild of Nuremberg, with the cobbler Hans Sachs (whom Wagner had come across through his earlier reading), as its central character. In a very short time, he completed the first prose draft of all three acts of *Die Meistersinger von Nürnberg*, though this task failed to exorcise the spell of *Lohengrin*. According to Wagner, he was sitting in a medicinal bath one day when he was overcome by a desire to begin work on the drama; and so he rushed home and started writing a prose scenario of *Lohengrin* at white heat, completing it by 3 August 1845. The final verse form was finished within a month of returning to Dresden and in December he read the libretto to a

Rosa Sucher and Gisela
Standigl in *Die Meistersinger*.

48

Lohengrin costume design.

small circle of friends and colleagues in the Engelklub. Among those present was Robert Schumann, who (supposedly) was disappointed that there were no arias or cavatinas written for individual singers, an opinion in keeping with his generally unfavourable view of Wagner's music.

The première of *Tannhäuser* took place in Dresden on 19 October 1845 and the opera soon became established as a firm favourite, with the public if not with the critics. With *Tannhäuser*, Wagner became fully aware of the direction in which his creative powers were leading him. He realised that only by uniting the poet and the composer in a single person could anything more of significance be achieved in opera. Despite the work's shortcomings (which Wagner readily acknowledged), *Tannhäuser* marks an advance in the development of Wagner's musical and dramatic technique, and also reflects his growing political awareness of the problems faced by the artist in society. The opera's profound originality was noted even by such usually hostile critics as Schumann, who wrote to the conductor Heinrich Dorn in 1846:

I wish you could see Wagner's *Tannhäuser*. It contains some deeply original material, definitely a hundred times better than his earlier operas – although some of it is still trivial. In short, he may turn out to be a great composer for the stage, and from what I know of him, he certainly has the courage. The technique and the orchestration I find outstanding, incomparably more masterly than before.

Wagner was never entirely happy with *Tannhäuser*, and kept revising the score from its first completion in 1845 to the last performance under his direction in 1875. At least four major 'versions' exist, of which the two best known (and widely performed) are the 'Dresden' version and the 'Paris' version of 1861, the latter of which is generally considered musically superior, though containing obvious stylistic discrepancies. Dissatisfied with some of the still-remaining traces of operatic tradition in *Tannhäuser*, Wagner kept planning new revisions right up to the last weeks of his life. 'I still owe *Tannhäuser* to the world,' he lamented to his wife, Cosima. Wagner was aware, while composing *Tannhäuser*, of the importance of the 'art of transition' to give the opera structural unity and cohesion, so vital in true music drama; and in the opera his use of transitional passages is certainly more sophisticated than in the *Holländer* – though one is still aware of formal numbers and set pieces in *Tannhäuser*, which lacks the flowing texture of *Lohengrin*. Similarly, although thematic ideas abound in the music, there is an absence of true *leitmotif* technique, an integral part of Wagner's compositional language from *Das Rheingold* onwards. Wagner expounded the

'Tannhäuser and Venus' by Delacroix.

principle of the *leitmotif*, or recurring *motif*, in his essay *Opera and Drama* (1851) – although he never actually used the expression. A *leitmotif* can be defined as a musical phrase associated with a particular character or idea, which grows out of the dramatic situation and is then developed (and usually modified) as a '*motif* of reminiscence' by the orchestra, so acting as a 'signpost for the emotions' throughout the remainder of the opera. In *Tannhäuser*, as in *Der fliegende Holländer*, there are strong melodic lines and examples of thematic recall, but the *leitmotifs* are not, as they are in the *Ring* operas, fully integrated into the symphonic texture.

Probably the greatest triumph of Wagner's career in Dresden was a performance he conducted of Beethoven's Choral Symphony on Palm Sunday, 5 April 1846, an event he organised despite furious resistance from the orchestral management and staff. The next month, Wagner and Minna retired to the picturesque village of Gross-Graupa, near Pillnitz, where he wrote the first musical draft of *Lohengrin*, completing the full orchestral score in Dresden nearly two years later, on 28 April 1848. During this time, while working on *Lohengrin*, Wagner immersed himself

50

in Germanic myth and Greek tragedy, as well as penning several political essays for left-wing journals. Of seminal importance to his future development were his studies of Aeschylus's *Oresteia* trilogy, Jakob Grimm's *Deutsche Mythologie* and various Nordic myths, all of which were to have a profound influence on the creation of the *Ring*.

In February 1847 Wagner scored another success with the

Richard Wagner.

production of his own revised version of Gluck's *Iphigenia in Aulis*, which confirmed his reputation as a sensitive interpreter of the German master. Less rewarding was the first Berlin performance of *Rienzi* in November 1847, which attracted unfavourable reviews from the critics and failed to secure from the King of Prussia a commission for a first performance of *Lohengrin*. To add to his misery, Wagner was refused a fee for the two months he had spent rehearsing the work, on the grounds that the management had only expressed a 'wish' and not issued an 'invitation'. Wagner's hopes of success, and even a post, in Berlin were finally dashed by this experience, and he became convinced that his work would never find acceptance while the existing social and political climate in Germany prevailed. 'As I travelled homeward with my wife,' he wrote in *Mein Leben*, 'through the bleak landscape of the Mark, I felt that the deep despair I was experiencing was a mood that I could be plunged into only once in a lifetime.'

After seeing *Tannhäuser* on to the stage Wagner spent three months compiling a report entitled *Concerning the Royal Orchestra*, which listed improvements he considered essential for bringing the orchestra up to strength. Wagner handed the report to Lüttichau in March 1846 but, despite its many sensible and practical suggestions, it was rejected a year later, probably because too many people felt threatened by the changes he proposed. In May 1848, Wagner produced another plan for theatrical reform, *On the Organisation of a German National Theatre for the Kingdom of Saxony*, which was also rejected by the court authorities. These experiences served to strengthen Wagner's growing political discontent, which was becoming indistinguishable from his frustration at having his artistic plans constantly thwarted. The musical establishment was so rooted in conventional taste that Wagner became convinced that only by changing the reactionary nature of society would his artistic aims ever be realised. Hounded mercilessly by creditors, mean-minded critics and imbecilic court officials, Wagner turned increasingly to subversive politics as the only way to achieve this change, and by 1848 he was more than ready to espouse the wave of revolutionary activity that was then about to break out in Germany.

7 Revolution and Exile

The period from the Congress of Vienna in 1815 to the revolutions of 1848 was characterised by growing resentment amongst the peoples of Europe against attempts by diplomats like Metternich to stifle the forces of change unleashed by Napoleon and the French Revolution. The territorial settlements imposed on the Great Powers at Vienna succeeded in keeping Europe free of large-scale wars for forty years, but on a national level these autocratic powers tried to repress the new ideas of the age, and by so doing caused the revolutionary explosion in 1848. By this time, poverty and repression were widespread, made worse by the bad harvest and business slump of 1847, which threw modern Europe into the worst depression it had ever known. Revolutionary thought flourished, particularly in France, where Louis Philippe had elevated the bourgeoisie to a position of great power at the expense of equality and the rights of man – the two most enduring legacies of the 1789 Revolution in the minds of the people.

On 12 January 1848 the people of Palermo in Sicily took to the streets in open revolt against Ferdinand II of Naples, and this set the pattern for a series of revolutions all over Europe within the course of the year. Most of these were nationalist and popular insurrections against foreign rule and, in the case of Austria and Germany, against the repressive policies of Metternich. In Germany in particular, the movement was based on a strong desire for national unity and an end to Austrian domination. The country did not have a tradition of violent revolutionary upheaval, like France, but its middle-class liberals had become outraged at the level of social deprivation that had grown up since 1815, a state of affairs that the sovereign princes of the German Confederation had done nothing to rectify.

Revolutionary hopes in Germany had been stirred by events in France in February 1848 (the same month that Karl Marx's *Communist Manifesto* was published in London), when the Paris mobs took to the streets and forced the abdication of Louis

Philippe. Paris had for some time been a hot-bed of socialist movements and theories, the leading thinkers being Saint-Simon, Charles Fourier and Pierre Proudhon, whose *De la propriété* (which expounded the idea that all property is theft) may have been familiar to Wagner from his Paris years. The uprising in Paris was soon followed by riots in Vienna, which forced the resignation of Metternich, and in Berlin. This first wave of revolutionary activity led to the formation of the Frankfurt Assembly, a representative body drawn from the different German states whose aim was to draw up a new German constitution. However, despite sitting for a whole year, the body became bogged down in disputes and did not even come close to realising the aspirations of its delegates for a liberal, united Germany. By the end of May 1848 the revolutionary fervour had died down, with nationalist movements remaining active only in Italy and Hungary. After the Berlin scare, Prussia, under Friedrich Wilhelm IV, was well on the way to further reactionary government; and in Germany as a whole the liberal movement had lost much of its impetus, not least because many of the prominent liberals of 1848 were professional men and intellectuals, who shied away from violent revolutionary solutions.

The year started badly for Wagner with the death of his mother on 9 January in Leipzig, a sad event which cut one of the last emotional links with his family. Up until the end of April 1848, while he was immersed in the composition of *Lohengrin*, the great events happening in Europe largely passed him by; and indeed he was still sceptical about the chances of a full-scale revolution taking place, even in France. However, he welcomed Friedrich August's appointment of a liberal government in Saxony in March – an enactment hastily put through after the people of Dresden had taken to the streets – and in May he confidently submitted his semi-political plan for a German National Theatre in Saxony, which was promptly turned down.

As all his schemes for theatrical reform were rejected, it was not long before Wagner moved on to overtly political acts in the hope of bringing about the changes in society he felt were so desperately needed. Although a visionary, Wagner was also a realist. As he became more and more disillusioned with the establishment – including the monarchy – he realised the need to combine his artistic beliefs with the political opportunities of the day, even though he was never in tune with the extremist theories of the hard-line revolutionaries. Also, although artistic reform was at the heart of his revolutionary fervour, Wagner had a history of espousing worthy causes going back to his student days. Although in *Mein Leben* he played down the part he played in the Dresden uprising (probably to please his new benefactor, King Ludwig), it

Friedrich August II of Saxony.

Mikhail Bakunin.

is likely that the events of 1848-9 stirred the idealist in him, as well as the man of action.

In June 1848 Wagner joined the revolutionary 'Vaterlands-verein', a leading republican group, and delivered a speech at an open-air meeting on the relation between republican aims and the monarchy. Money was denounced as the root of all evil, as it fostered such un-Christian practices as public and private usury – a subject close to Wagner's heart. He praised the Saxon House of Wettin, and appealed to the king to place himself at the head of the new republic (an idea in keeping with the desire of bourgeois liberals for constitutional government rather than communism), but his attack on the privileged court aristocracy became the talk of the town for days afterwards, and Wagner was fortunate not to have been summarily dismissed.

Through his friend August Röckel, the publisher of the republican journal the *Volksblätter* (to which Wagner contributed several anonymous articles), he was introduced to Mikhail Bakunin, the Russian anarchist, whose ceaseless energy and fearsome doctrines fascinated Wagner, although their politics were, in reality, poles apart. Wagner could not agree with Bakunin's extremist arguments, especially regarding the destruction of all cultural institutions; and Bakunin in turn regarded Wagner as a 'dreamer'. However, despite the fact that Wagner referred to Bakunin in *Mein Leben* as a 'confused hothead', there is no doubt that in the heady days of 1848-9 he was a willing receptacle for Bakunin's revolutionary sermonising. Overall, it is difficult to say from where or from whom Wagner picked up his knowledge of extreme political theory, especially as it is unclear which books he read on the subject (although it has been shown that his library contained no political texts). However, through his friendship with men like Bakunin, Lehrs and Röckel he must have had many heated discussions in the smoke-filled rooms of Dresden on the political writers of the day, such as Proudhon, Ludwig Feuerbach, Max Stirner, Karl Marx and Friedrich Engels, and some of the theories he gleaned from these discussions found their way into his *Volksblätter* articles and into his later *Ring* operas.

Wagner's conception of *Der Ring des Nibelungen* (The Ring of the Nibelung) began to take shape in the autumn of 1848, when he completed a prose outline of a large part of the plot of the *Ring*, entitled *The Nibelung Myth as the Sketch for a Drama*. From this, he wrote the libretto *Siegfried's Tod* (Siegfried's Death), which later became *Götterdämmerung*, the final opera in the *Ring* cycle. At the same time Wagner was toying with a project he had begun in 1846, for a five-act work based on the twelfth-century emperor Frederick Barbarossa, entitled *Friedrich I*. Although in *Mein*

The Dresden uprising, 1849.

Leben Wagner said that he abandoned the Barbarossa project when he realised that myth had greater dramatic potential than history, it seems certain that the writing of *Friedrich I* and *Siegfried's Tod* overlapped, so that the genesis of the *Ring* was not quite the revelation he wished posterity to believe. Indeed, in January 1849, just two months after completing *Siegfried's Tod*, Wagner began work on another drama, *Jesus von Nazareth*, which reflects some of the revolutionary thinking of the time. This project was also abandoned, although it was not until 1851, after some vacillating, that Wagner made up his mind definitely to compose the *Ring*.

As he became more and more involved in subversive politics, Wagner took little interest in his official court duties and the management began to regard him with increasing suspicion. The final straw for Wagner came when Lüttichau, without a word of explanation, abruptly cancelled the impending production of *Lohengrin*, for which the sets had already been ordered. From that moment, wrote Wagner, 'I turned my back on the theatre and on every attempt to interest myself in it.' In 1849, however, events in Germany took a dramatic new turn, and Wagner's fate became caught up in the general political maelstrom. In March, the dilatory Frankfurt Assembly finally decided to offer the imperial crown of a united Germany to the King of Prussia, but Friedrich Wilhelm IV, now politically secure in his own state, rejected the

56

offer and, along with Austria, withdrew from the Assembly. In Saxony, as elsewhere, Friedrich August II repudiated the constitution agreed at Frankfurt and dissolved both Chambers of Parliament. This action brought the populace of Dresden to boiling point and, in expectation of an uprising, Prussian troops were called in to assist the King's own army. On hearing this news, the crowds took to the streets, barricades were erected, and shots were fired by the Saxon soldiers. Wagner had leaflets printed with the words 'Are you with us against the foreign troops?' which, at great personal risk to himself, he distributed to the soldiers during a cease-fire. Moves were also afoot to arm the populace and Wagner may have instructed a brass-founder to manufacture hand grenades.

The fighting started in earnest on 5 May, and Wagner spent that night on top of the tower of the Kreuzkirche observing troop movements, while under the constant hail of Prussian bullets. The militia of the recently formed provisional government were no match for the disciplined Prussian troops, and by the morning of 9 May the insurrection had collapsed. Clara Schumann noted in her diary some of the terrible events that ensued:

On Thursday the 10th we heard of the awful atrocities committed by the troops; they shot down every insurgent they could find, and our landlady told us that her brother, an innkeeper, was made to stand and watch while the soldiers shot twenty-six students they found in a room there, one after the other. Then, so it is said, they hurled men into the street by the dozen from the third and fourth floors.

The authorities soon began to round up the ringleaders, and Röckel and Bakunin were arrested and sentenced to death, commuted to life imprisonment. (Röckel spent the next thirteen years in jail, and Bakunin was sent back to Russia, from where he fled in 1861.) Wagner would undoubtedly have suffered the same fate as his two friends, but thanks to a fortunate accident he avoided arrest and escaped. While en route to Chemnitz with Bakunin and the other members of the provisional government, Wagner became separated from the party, and arrived in the town independently, spending the night alone in an inn. Oblivious of the fact that his comrades had walked into a trap, Wagner left Chemnitz the next day and made his way to Weimar, where his friend Franz Liszt, the composer (whom he had first met in Paris in 1840), was more than ready to give him shelter and practical assistance. However, a warrant for Wagner's arrest was issued on 16 May and he realised he would have to leave Germany without delay. Liszt urged him to make for Paris, where perhaps his genius would at last be recognised; and so Wagner – although with considerable misgivings as to the choice of destination – took leave of his wife at Jena and set off once again for France, without realising that he would be exiled from his homeland for the next eleven years.

Because he was a wanted man in Germany (and travelling on a false passport), Wagner was advised to take the longer route to Paris, via Switzerland. On 29 May 1849 he arrived in Zürich, and upon seeing the magnificent scenery of the lakes and the Swiss Alps, Wagner immediately resolved to seek permission to settle there. In fact, Wagner's residency in Switzerland was to cover a period of over twenty-three years and it was there, under the gaze of the mountains, that he composed the *Ring*, *Tristan und Isolde* and *Die Meistersinger*, as well as some of his most significant critical writings. Wagner's initial good impression of Zürich was no doubt helped by the sympathetic reception he received from the inhabitants of the town. 'To my complete amazement,' he wrote to his friend Theodor Uhlig, 'I find that I am famous here, thanks to arrangements of all my operas, whole acts of which have been frequently performed at concerts and by music societies.' However, to please Liszt and Minna, he obtained a new Swiss passport (which, interestingly, gives his height as 5ft 6½ins), and proceeded, full of foreboding, to Paris.

The city at that time was in the grip of the terrible cholera epidemic that was sweeping through Europe, claiming hundreds of lives every day. To complement the funereal atmosphere, there was political tension in the streets as the Assembly took measures to prevent further revolutionary disturbance. After the Revolution of 1848, the monarchy had been replaced by the Second Republic, of which Louis Napoleon, nephew of Napoleon I, had been elected president. Louis Napoleon's *coup d'état* in December 1851, in which he dissolved the Assembly and later declared himself Emperor, saw the return of the barricades and further bloodshed; but the protest was short-lived and, under Napoleon's dictatorial grip, Paris in the 1850s and 60s settled into an era of unsurpassed gaiety that soon made the city the unrivalled Mecca for the pleasure-seekers of Europe. To Wagner, however, Paris was just as base, vulgar and artistically redundant as when he had last been there and in July, after an unproductive stay, he returned to Zürich.

During the rest of 1849, Wagner wrote two essays, *Art and Revolution* and *The Artwork of the Future*, the first of an important series of critical writings completed during his time in Zürich which contributed to his growing fame (and notoriety) in Europe from 1850 onwards. In these essays Wagner attempted to create a new artistic ideal, and hopefully precipitate the revolution in opera (and society) that was needed before the 'artwork of the

58

future' could come into being. The Greek experience – in particular, Greek tragedy – provided the model for this ideal, for only here were the different elements of poetry, drama, music and dance combined to make a unified artwork, created by, and for, the people (*das Volk*). With its emphasis on frivolity and spectacle, the nineteenth-century theatre had reached a point furthest away from the Greek achievement, so that only by revolution could the 'total work of art' (*Gesamtkunstwerk*) fulfil its essential role as the creative expression of a free humanity. The theoretical basis of Wagnerian music drama was further explained in his next major essay, *Opera and Drama* (1851), in which he expounded the structural significance of the leitmotif 'in the shaping of the drama of the future' – a theory that was soon to be vindicated in the musical composition of the *Ring*, which he was by then working over in his mind.

Minna arrived in Zürich in September 1849 and immediately began pressing Wagner to seek his fortune in Paris once again.

Before leaving, he heard the very welcome news that an admirer of his, Frau Julie Ritter, the mother of his friend Karl Ritter, planned to make him an annual allowance of 800 thalers. Furthermore, a young friend of hers, Jessie Laussot, who had once visited Wagner in Dresden and who was now married to a Bordeaux wine merchant, Eugène Laussot, wished to increase this allowance by a further 2500 francs. This good fortune did not sway Minna from her purpose, however, and on 29 January 1850 Wagner left for Paris for the third time, armed with the recently completed prose draft of an opera, *Wieland der Schmied* (Wieland the Smith), which he hoped would appeal to French taste. In Paris, Wagner came up against the same brick wall as before; and his disappointment at the rejection of *Wieland der Schmied* by the Opéra was aggravated by the fact that Meyerbeer had just scored another triumph with his new opera, *La Prophète*. 'I am ill and my illness is called Paris,' he wrote to his friend Jakob Sulzer.

At the beginning of March, events took an unexpected course when he received an invitation from the Laussots to visit them in Bordeaux, where he and Jessie very quickly discovered a strong mutual attraction. As well as being an ardent admirer of his work, Jessie Laussot was young, attractive and gifted. During enraptured evenings together, he read her the texts of *Siegfried's Tod* and *Wieland der Schmied*, and she played Beethoven for him on the piano. Both felt unhappily married and, with the recklessness of new lovers, they promised to abandon their respective spouses and elope together to Greece or the Middle East. Wagner returned to Paris, where he wrote Minna a decisive letter of farewell, and worked out a plan of escape. Unfortunately, Jessie made the mistake of informing her mother of the impending elopement and she promptly informed Eugène, who threatened to put a bullet into his rival. Undeterred, Wagner hastened to Bordeaux, only to find that Eugène had taken his household off to the country and alerted the local police to be on the lookout for him. Minna generously welcomed him back, though she was deeply hurt by the affair. However, the lesson of the Laussot episode had been learnt and she never again coerced him into making a career in Paris.

Fuelled by rekindled loathing for Paris, and particularly for Meyerbeer's new opera, Wagner wrote his most notorious, and self-damaging essay, *Jewishness in Music*, which was published in August 1850 in the *Neue Zeitschrift für Musik*, under the pseudonym K. Freigedank. In the controversy that has always surrounded this article, attention has been paid not to Wagner's often perceptively argued analysis of the place of the Jewish artist in society, but rather to his personal malice against Jews in the theatre world (especially successful ones), and to the contribution

Siegfried's death,
Götterdämmerung Act III.

the article made to the long and shameful tradition of anti-semitism in German thought and literature – a tradition that was to lead inexorably to the Third Reich and the Holocaust. In its conception, *Jewishness in Music* was very much tied up with Meyerbeer at whom, as Wagner admitted in a letter to Liszt, the article was aimed, even though it did not mention his name. Despite some scurrilous theorising about the Jews being deracinated aliens who were artistically superficial and obsessed with money and status, the real motivation for Wagner's racism probably stems from his frustration at being rejected by a society which lionised Meyerbeer and his kind. As he had been reduced to beg Meyerbeer for help on many occasions, an attack on him (and, for added spite, on his race) would be an assertion, albeit an anonymous one, of his determination to divorce himself, both personally and artistically, from this 'dishonest relationship', and so exorcise the envy and self-hatred that had grown out of his failure to succeed as an independent artist.

On 28 August 1850 Liszt conducted the première of *Lohengrin* at Weimar which, although a success with the public, convinced Wagner of the inadequacy of the conventional theatre for the staging of his works. In a letter to his friend Ernst Benedikt Kietz, he first mentioned the idea of building a festival theatre to his own design, which would employ the best singers to give ideal performances of his works. He estimated the cost at not less than 10,000 thalers. 'If Karl Ritter's uncle dies I shall get the money!' he wrote cheerfully. However, in spite of Wagner's practical reservations, the performances of *Lohengrin* at Weimar showed that his operas could be staged, given even limited resources, and after 1850 they were in constant demand by provincial theatres all over Germany.

Lohengrin was Wagner's last 'Romantic opera' which, although retaining the vestiges – both dramatic and musical – of traditional opera, stands poised on the brink of music drama. In particular, the masterly orchestration, the sophisticated harmonic technique and the close relationship between the music, the text and the visual action represent a considerable stylistic leap from the more formally conventional *Tannhäuser*. This advance is in evidence from the beginning, in the hauntingly beautiful A major Prelude which, in its treatment of thematic ideas from the opera, is a long way from the traditional overture that had been the norm since the middle of the eighteenth century. The chorus was also used to far greater dramatic effect than in his earlier operas and some of the principal *motifs* – especially that of the Forbidden Question – have a musico-poetic significance within the structure of the opera that anticipates the full use of the *leitmotif* process in the *Ring*.

Wagner's attempts in the early months of 1851 to set *Siegfried's*

Title-page of the *Lohengrin* poem, 1850.

Tod to music ran into difficulties and he got no further than composition sketches for the Norns' scene. Wagner soon realised that in order to understand the full significance of the *motifs* – which, as outlined in *Opera and Drama*, should be associative and modifiable – more mythic background was needed in which the themes could be first introduced and developed. In this way, if a *motif* representing a particular idea or object is played by the orchestra during, say, the Norns' scene, then the audience should immediately associate that *motif* with what has previously been heard in the text or seen on the stage – in other words, it becomes a '*motif* of reminiscence' which can make its own comment on what is happening at any point in the drama. On a structural level, the *motifs* in the *Ring* extend like a web across the entire fabric of the four operas, all developed out of a small number of initial *motifs* that are unceasingly varied and modified, so that everything is linked together in a network of unbroken, 'infinite melody'. In 1851, Wagner realised that this was the compositional technique to which his previous creative efforts had been leading, and that he needed to write another drama to precede *Siegfried's Tod* if he was to evolve a system of *leitmotifs* that would fully reflect the mythic and epic nature of the *Ring*. Therefore, in May and June he wrote the prose draft and libretto of *Der junge Siegfried* (later called *Siegfried*). Later that year, he decided to enlarge the two-part drama to a four-part one, to encompass the whole myth as mapped out in 1848 in *The Nibelung Myth as Sketch for a Drama*; and with the librettos of *Das Rheingold* and *Die Walküre*, the text of the entire *Ring* was completed by 15 December 1852.

Wagner took the opportunity, with the publication of the texts of his three previous operas by Breitkopf & Härtel in August 1851, to write a long autobiographical preface entitled *A Communication to my Friends*, in which he explained the reasons for his move away from romantic opera towards a new concept of mythical drama. In September, Wagner went to Albisbrunn, near Zürich, to take a severe course of water-cure for his gastric problems. It was here, while pondering on the music for his two 'Siegfried' texts, that he decided on the final *Ring* scheme of three dramas with a prologue (*Das Rheingold*). By the time he returned to Zürich in November 1851, he had written the prose sketches of *Das Rheingold* and *Die Walküre*, explaining in a letter to Liszt that the expansion of the original idea had been forced upon him as the necessary consequence of the nature of the material. Liszt encouraged him by comparing his task to that of the cathedral architect in Seville, who was told to '"Build us a temple such that future generations will surely say that the chapter was mad to undertake something so extraordinary." And yet the cathedral still stands!'

Das Rheingold, published by Breitkopf & Hartel.

Despite the good news of having his annual allowance of 800 thalers confirmed at this time by Frau Julie Ritter (an allowance he continued to receive until 1859), Wagner's spirits were considerably dampened by news of Louis Napoleon's *coup d'état* in Paris on 2 December 1851. With the *Ring* in its infancy, Wagner still fervently believed that a social revolution was needed to create the right climate for his work, as can be seen from his letters to his friends Theodor Uhlig and Ernst Kiétz dating from this period (some of which were later censored by Cosima), in which he states that only out of the ruins of 'the most fearful and destructive of revolutions' can the right artists and audiences be found. The writing of the librettos of *Das Rheingold* and *Die Walküre* (in reverse order) was completed in May-November 1852. In the light of these two dramas, Wagner had to make changes to *Der junge Siegfried* and *Siegfried's Tod* (the names were not officially changed to *Siegfried* and *Götterdämmerung* until 1863), the most significant of which was the ending, where instead of being allowed to reign in glory, Wotan and the gods are destroyed when Valhalla comes crashing down in flames. The revisions were finished by December and, in February 1853, on four successive evenings at the Hotel Baur au Lac in Zürich, Wagner read the entire *Ring* poem to a rapt audience.

While in Zürich, Wagner was introduced to various wealthy and influential people who were willing to give him help and financial assistance, the most munificent of these being Otto Wesendonck, a successful silk merchant, whom Wagner met in February 1852. Wesendonck generously extricated Wagner from debt crises on more than one occasion; and in the person of his young wife, Mathilde, Wagner found the perfect muse, who provided him with encouragement, inspiration and love. He quickly became infatuated with Mathilde and out of their famous relationship grew Wagner's towering monument to love, *Tristan*

Hotel Baur au Lac, Zurich.

und Isolde. In the same year, Wagner met François and Eliza Wille, at whose charming house at Mariafeld he would often seek refuge from his financial and marital troubles.

By 1853, having completed the *Ring* poem, Wagner was anxious to start work on the musical composition, but his difficulties were compounded by his never having heard a performance of any part of *Lohengrin* other than the finale of the first act. 'I must hear *Lohengrin* once,' he wrote to Liszt. 'Until I have, I do not want, nor am I able, to make music again!' Therefore, with Wesendonck's help, Wagner organised three special concerts of excerpts from *Rienzi*, *Holländer*, *Tannhäuser* and *Lohengrin*, the last of which took place on 22 May 1853 – his fortieth birthday. The concerts, which in effect represented the first 'Wagner Festival', were a great success and Wagner confessed to Liszt that 'There is a certain beautiful woman at whose feet I laid the entire festival.'

As a conductor, Wagner was held in high esteem in Zürich, especially for his exciting interpretations of Beethoven's symphonies and Mozart's operas; but his steadily increasing reputation both as a performer and a composer failed to bring in the hoped-for funds, and his debts rose inexorably (by September 1854 he estimated them at 10,000 francs). As well as his increasing insolvency, Wagner also had his unhappy marital situation to contend with. Minna, as ever, had little sympathy with his artistic aims, and her worsening heart condition made her even more irritable and intolerant.

Increasingly depressed with his lot, Wagner felt that he needed some creative peace in order to begin the gigantic task of composing the *Ring*; and so, in August 1853 he set out for Italy, hoping to find inspiration in a fresh, untroubled environment. After visiting Turin and Genoa, Wagner booked into an inn in the coastal town of La Spezia where, on the evening of 5 September, as he lay on his couch in a kind of half-sleep, he claims he had a 'vision' of the music of *Das Rheingold*:

I suddenly got the feeling that I was sinking into a strong current of water. Its rushing soon developed into a musical sound as the chord of E flat major, surging incessantly in broken chords; these presented themselves as melodic figurations of increasing motion, but the pure chord of E flat major never altered, seeming by its persistence to give the element into which I was sinking an infinite significance. With the sensation that the waves were now flowing high above me I woke with a violent start from my half-sleep. I recognised immediately that the orchestral prelude to *Das Rheingold* had come to me, as I had borne it in me but had been unable to find exactly . . . (*Mein Leben*)‡

‡ Translated by Mary Whittall, reproduced from Curt von Westernhagen, *Wagner: A Biography*.

Whether or not this is another of Wagner's apocryphal claims designed to give a mystical significance to past events will probably never be proved one way or the other. It is clear, however, that Wagner considered La Spezia to be a watershed in his career and as soon as he returned to Zürich on 1 November he began to sketch the music of the prelude, starting with the primordial sound of the E flat major triad over a sustained pedal point, which, as he once commented to Liszt, suggested 'the beginning of the world'. The composition sketch of *Das Rheingold* was written in just nine weeks, and the full score was completed on 26 September 1854, by which time work on the second of the *Ring* operas, *Die Walküre*, was well under way.

Heinrich Vogl as Loge in *Das Rheingold*.

8 Tristan

Arthur Schopenhauer.

In the autumn of 1854 Georg Herwegh, one of Wagner's old revolutionary friends, introduced him to Arthur Schopenhauer's *Die Welt als Wille und Vorstellung* (The World as Will and Idea), a book that was to have a seminal influence on his creative development. Wagner read it four times during the next year, and throughout his life he remained a fervent admirer of Schopenhauer, even though the two men never met. Wagner never tired of discussing Schopenhauer's philosophy and recommending the book to his friends, and he even attempted to establish a chair of Schopenhauerian philosophy at Zürich University. By this time an old man and set in his ways, Schopenhauer's musical tastes remained true to Mozart and Rossini, and Wagner's admiration was never reciprocated. At Christmas 1854, Wagner sent him one of the fifty special copies of the *Ring* poem he had had printed, on which Schopenhauer scribbled disapproving notes in the margins commenting sourly to François Wille that 'the man's a poet, not a musician'.

Wagner was affected both by Schopenhauer's aesthetics and by his pessimistic philosophy of life; and the fact that the text of the *Ring* (written *before* he discovered *Die Welt als Wille und Vorstellung*) is often profoundly Schopenhauerian bears witness to the amazing affinity that existed between the minds of the two men. Schopenhauer held that the world is a mirror of the Will, which he used to mean the essence, or inner nature, of everything (rather than the usual sense of the word, as meaning personal determination). Human beings, with their limited perceptions, can claim no knowledge of this 'ultimate reality', other than when the 'Will' manifests itself as material 'phenomena'. The world, and all the individuals in it, are therefore, 'Will, through and through', and the attempts by humanity to attach significance to the world of appearances, while denying the essential unity of all things, is the basis of the one truly tragic world view. Schopenhauer's aesthetics were complemented by his pessimistic

Minna Wagner.

outlook on life, which concluded that the tragic individual, burdened by constant striving and inevitable suffering, eventually renounces the will-to-live ('the Will thus freely annuls itself') and yields up his life – a concept that Wagner had already embodied in *Der fliegende Holländer* and repeated in the *Ring*, *Tristan und Isolde* and *Parsifal*.

If Schopenhauer's theory of tragic resignation was already familiar to Wagner, as expressed poetically in the persons of the Dutchman and Wotan, it was his assertion in *Die Welt als Wille und Vorstellung* that music alone was able to articulate the 'Will' (*ie* express the essence of things, or the 'absolute' qualities, such as Joy, Grief or Love) that convinced Wagner of the greater potential of music over other art forms. By the time he composed *Tristan* and *Götterdämmerung*, the music had become elevated to a role of much higher importance in expressing, through the orchestra, the feelings and emotions experienced by the characters. Wagner does, however, diverge from Schopenhauer's teachings in his belief in the possibility of redemption, or salvation, through love, which continues to exist as a transforming force even after the world of appearances has vanished.

It was just after reading Schopenhauer for the first time that Wagner, by then deeply involved with Mathilde Wesendonck, conceived the idea of writing *Tristan und Isolde*. In a letter to Liszt dated 16 December 1854 he said that as he 'had never in his life enjoyed the true happiness of love', he wanted to 'raise a monument to this loveliest of all dreams'. Just how much this operatic idealisation of love is a dramatisation of his (probably platonic) affair with Mathilde Wesendonck is hard to qualify. Wagner later stated that the writing of *Tristan und Isolde* had been 'divorced from experience and reality'; although it is fair to say that the combination of his new-found love, and Schopenhauer's metaphysics, represented the moving forces behind *Tristan*, and they kindled the creative idea that was probably already brooding within him. At the end of 1854, however, Wagner was immersed in the composition sketch of the final act of *Die Walküre* and so his urge to write *Tristan* had to be held at bay. He eventually started work on the prose draft in August 1857, after breaking off the composition of the *Ring*, a decision probably dictated by pressing financial considerations as well as by the promptings of his Muse.

In January 1855 Wagner accepted an invitation by the 'Old' Philharmonic Society to conduct eight concerts in London, at a fee of £200. Although, as he confessed to Liszt, the prospect filled him with gloom, he realised that a success in London would certainly help to bolster his reputation in Europe and he welcomed the idea of once again working with a well-trained orchestra. However, his four-month stay in England more than confirmed his original

Prince Albert and Queen
Victoria.

apprehension. The weather was foggy and depressing, the concert programmes were arbitrarily put together, one rehearsal only per concert was allowed, the audiences showed a complete lack of discrimination, and the critics were viciously hostile. Suffering from ill health throughout his visit, he spent despondent mornings in his house near Regent's Park trying to score the first two acts of *Die Walküre*, although his concentration was affected by his bad mood. In the afternoons he plunged into Dante's *Inferno*, which seemed to take on an awful reality in the grey atmosphere of London. In a letter to Liszt, he compared his existence to that of 'one of the damned in Hell'.

Wagner's stay in London did have some highlights, however. The seventh concert of the series (on 11 June) was attended by Queen Victoria and Prince Albert, who asked for an encore of the *Tannhäuser* overture and received Wagner in their box during the interval, where they had an animated conversation about opera. Wagner also renewed the acquaintance of Berlioz, who was in

Illustration of scene from *Die Walküre* by Ferdinand Leeke.

London to conduct the 'New' Philharmonic. He was saddened by the older composer's apparent world weariness and, although Wagner had an ambivalent attitude to Berlioz's music, both men had suffered shameful neglect in France and shared an antipathy towards the contemporary musical scene. He had a less rewarding experience when, quite by chance, he bumped into Meyerbeer, the two men astonishing onlookers by coldly walking past each other without a word. Wagner's frequent companion in London was Ferdinand Praeger, a German music teacher who, after Wagner's death, published a book entitled *Wagner as I Knew Him*, which was later proven to be such a tissue of lies that the publishers were obliged to withdraw it. Through Praeger, Wagner also met Karl Klindworth, a young pupil of Liszt, who later became the adoptive father of Winifred Williams, the wife of Wagner's son (by Cosima), Siegfried.

Despite making a few useful acquaintanceships, Wagner's stay in London was unproductive, both creatively and financially. The cost of living in London was high and, by the time he left in June 1855, he had managed to save only 1,000 francs, which represented 'the hardest money I have ever earned in my life'. His experiences in London further convinced him of his alienation from the artistic activities of Europe, and he inwardly cursed the illusion of success that kept leading his judgement astray. Weary with the struggle, he returned to Zürich, 'with a feeling of bitterness such as I hope I shall never again experience'.

The exhausting task of scoring the remainder of *Die Walküre* was completed by March 1856, by which time Wagner's health, marriage and finances were all seriously in decline. His erysipelas plagued him remorselessly, relations with Minna were unimproved, and his dependence on Otto Wesendonck for support was complicated by his growing love for Wesendonck's wife, Mathilde. With his troubles piling up in Zürich, Wagner's thoughts turned once again to Germany, where he hoped eventually to have the *Ring* performed. However, the new King of Saxony, Johann, had not forgotten Wagner's part in the uprising of 1848 and, although he was to grant him a full amnesty in 1862, in 1856 Wagner was still very much *persona non grata*, who was possibly still under surveillance by the authorities. Wagner seriously believed that the Dresden court was over-reacting to his so-called revolutionary activities which, he reasoned, had a purely artistic purpose devoid of any criminal intention towards the King. However, after seven years of exile, he felt it was time to swallow his pride and address a plea to King Johann; and so in May 1856 he wrote him a letter acknowledging, for the first time, his guilt in 'deserting the proper sphere of art for the field of politics' and promising never again to indulge in such activities.

Mathilde Wesendonck and her son.

View of Zurich, showing the Wesendonck's villa on the left.

The King passed the letter to the Ministry of Justice, and in August Wagner was informed that his petition had been unequivocally rejected.

On the same day that he wrote to the King of Saxony, Wagner made a prose sketch for a drama based on a Buddhist legend, called *Die Sieger* (The Victors). Indian culture had interested him for some time, and he felt an instinctive sympathy with the doctrines of Buddhism, which had many points of contact with Schopenhauer's philosophy. Dealing with the themes of renunciation and redemption, *Die Sieger* was not developed any further as a drama in its own right, although its preoccupations eventually found their way into *Parsifal*. After finishing *Die Walküre*, a task that had drained him physically and emotionally, Wagner was anxious to get his health in order before beginning the composition of *Siegfried*. Suffering constantly from attacks of erysipelas, he was recommended to consult a Dr Vaillant who ran a hydropathic clinic near Geneva. The régime there was considerably milder than some of the other water tortures Wagner had endured in the past and, to his great relief, the treatment was successful.

Wagner realised that he needed peace and quiet to complete the *Ring*, and while at Dr Vaillant's establishment he devoted his time to designing a house for himself, which he hoped to build from the proceeds of the publication of the work. He proposed to Breitkopf & Härtel that a fee of 10,000 thalers would not be unreasonable for 'the most important work of my life'; but, with a remarkable lack of foresight, the publishers turned down the offer, thereby losing themselves a fortune. This rejection was a great blow to Wagner and he despaired of ever finding the tranquillity, or money, needed to finish the *Ring*. 'The little house I have for so long been yearning for as a quiet place to work,' he wrote to Princess Wittgenstein, Liszt's companion, 'is still nothing but a castle in the sky, probably next door to Valhalla.' Fortunately, at this point Otto Wesendonck stepped in with the offer of the tenancy of a small house adjacent to a villa he was having built for himself in a suburb of Zürich, where Wagner would be able to continue his work untroubled by the world. Wagner moved into the house the following spring and called it his 'Asyl' (Sanctuary).

Filled with renewed optimism by Wesendonck's generous offer, in September 1856 Wagner began the composition sketch of *Siegfried*, although by this time the music of *Tristan* was never far from his thoughts. Despite the interruption of a long visit from Liszt and Princess Wittgenstein, who managed to turn the normally staid Zürich social scene into a glittering affair worthy of Paris, Wagner completed the score of Act I of *Siegfried* by the end of March 1857. On 28 April, he and Minna moved into the Asyl, which soon began to exert a beneficial influence over him. In *Mein Leben*, Wagner stated that when sitting one sunny day on the verandah of the Asyl, it suddenly occurred to him that it was Good

Below:
Otto Wesendonck.

The 'Asyl', pencil drawing by G. Meyer.

Friday, which immediately made him think of Wolfram's *Parsifal*. Since reading the poem in Marienbad, he had not given it a second thought; but now, he claimed, struck by the significance of that holy day, he rapidly made a prose sketch of a new three-act drama. Unfortunately, poetic as it may be, this appears to be one of Wagner's more tendentious claims, as that year Good Friday fell on 10 April, *before* Wagner moved into the Asyl. He later admitted to Cosima (recorded in her Diaries of April 1879) that the *Mein Leben* version of events was merely the result of a 'pleasant mood in Nature', which made him think, 'This is how a Good Friday ought to be'.

By this time, Wagner had been working on the *Ring*, on and off, for nine years and it was still nowhere near completion. Financial considerations were now pressing, and he realised that he must produce something readily performable on a conventional stage if he was not to end up forgotten as well as bankrupt. He made one last attempt to interest Breitkopf & Härtel in the *Ring* and, following their second refusal, he reluctantly decided to abandon the 'stubborn exercise' of finishing the Nibelung drama and turn his attention to *Tristan und Isolde*. On 28 June 1857 he wrote to Liszt: 'I have led my young Siegfried into the beautiful forest solitude; there I have left him under a linden tree and, with tears from the depths of my heart, have bade him farewell.' Wagner in fact continued working on the composition sketch of Act II up to the end of July, and then put aside the composition of Act III until March 1869, a gap of twelve years.

As well as his need for money, Wagner may well have had other, artistic, reasons for abandoning the *Ring* in 1857. Clearly, the colossal task ahead of him seemed even more forbidding after his disappointment with his publishers, especially as no immediate prospect existed of the work ever being performed. He feared that with the *Ring* he had entered the realms of the 'unstageable and the unsingable', and that what was needed was 'a manageable and thoroughly practicable opera' which would appeal to provincial theatres and so enable him to re-establish contact with the musical public. (As it turned out, *Tristan* took two years to write and, because of the difficulty of the work, another six before it was staged.) Also, Wagner may genuinely have felt that he had written himself to a standstill so far as the *Ring* was concerned. In hindsight, it is clear that *Götterdämmerung* would not have existed in the form it does if Wagner had not first composed *Tristan* and *Die Meistersinger*.

The complexity of the score of *Tristan* is telling enough evidence that forces were at work in Wagner which outweighed any practical considerations, however pressing, when he tearfully took his leave of Siegfried in the forest solitude. As early as 1854 he mentioned to Liszt the idea of writing *Tristan*, and there is evidence that some of the music existed before the text was written. At the end of 1856 Wagner told Princess Marie Wittgenstein that while composing *Siegfried* he had 'slipped unawares' into *Tristan*: 'music without words for the present'. Also, a musical sketch from around this time which Wagner sent to Mathilde Wesendonck includes the four chromatically rising notes from the prelude which lie at the heart of the opera's conception. With this new musical language welling inside him, all that was required was the intervention of external forces – his need for money, his love for Mathilde Wesendonck, and his immersion in Schopenhauer – to provide the necessary impetus to bring *Tristan* to fruition. In seeking a new language to express the obsessive love and yearning of Tristan and Isolde, Wagner created a revolutionary synthesis of sound which jolted harmonic theory out of the classical and into the modern era. Regarded with incomprehension by most of his contemporaries, the extreme chromaticism and daringly innovative harmony and orchestration of *Tristan* represented a milestone in the evolution of modern music and a sublime testament to Wagner's dramatic vision.

Wagner began the prose sketch of *Tristan* at the Asyl on 20 August 1857, two days before the Wesendoncks moved into

Hans von Bülow.

74

their new villa, and the poem was completed on 18 September. A few days after this an extraordinary meeting took place in the Asyl. The pianist Hans von Bülow and his nineteen-year-old bride Cosima (the illegitimate daughter of Liszt and the Comtesse d'Agoult) were visiting Zurich on their honeymoon and Wagner invited them to stay at his house for a few weeks. Bülow impressed Wagner by his sight-reading of the first two acts of *Siegfried* and his mastery of the piano. (In spite of the anguish he was to suffer at Wagner's hands, Bülow remained a devoted admirer in the troubled years ahead, conducting the première of *Tristan* in 1865.) One evening Wagner read the *Tristan* poem to the assembled gathering, which included Minna, Mathilde and Cosima – his wife, his lover, and his future wife – together with both their husbands, a singular occasion that must have been fraught with emotional tension. Wagner and Mathilde had recently declared their undying love for each other, and her tearful response to the last act of *Tristan* must have aroused the suspicions of all those present in the room.

During the time Wagner was composing the music of Act I of *Tristan* (1 October-31 December 1857), Mathilde's visits to the Asyl were becoming more and more frequent. Between November 1857 and May 1858 he set five of Mathilde's poems to music, one

Liszt's children, Cosima, Blandine and Daniel.

of the very rare occasions he worked with somebody else's text. The songs became known as the *Wesendonck Lieder* and they are steeped in the harmonies of *Tristan*. As the lovers' trysts were naively indiscreet, it became clear to Minna and Otto that a full-blown affair was in progress right under their noses. Things came to a head in January 1858 following a row between the Wesendoncks, and to avert a crisis Wagner thought it best to take himself off to Paris for a few weeks to let tempers cool down.

Shortly after his return to Zürich, he and Mathilde had a falling-out one evening over a trifling artistic matter, at the root of which was Wagner's jealousy of her handsome Italian language teacher. The next day (7 April 1858), feeling guilty at letting his baser instincts get the better of him, Wagner sent Mathilde a conciliatory letter tucked into a pencil sketch of the *Tristan* prelude which, unfortunately, was intercepted by Minna before it reached its destination. Minna furiously confronted her husband with the letter, which she took to be proof of his infidelity, and then brandished it in front of Mathilde with the threat: 'If I were any ordinary woman I would go to your husband with this letter.' With passions running high, Wagner, not wishing to put his tenancy of the Asyl in jeopardy, but also worried about Minna's worsening heart condition, decided temporarily to cool his relations with Mathilde. Shortly afterwards the Wesendoncks left for a change of air in Italy, and Minna went to Brestenberg Sanatorium, near Zürich, to receive treatment for her ailments.

By the time Minna returned in July 1858 Wagner had written the composition sketch of Act II of *Tristan*, completed in an atmosphere of dreamlike seclusion. With all the protagonists in the real-life drama now back at their respective homes, battle was rejoined, with both women bitter and reproachful towards Wagner and refusing to speak to each other. Life in the Asyl was now 'a hell from which I daily long to be released', Wagner wrote to Eliza Wille, and he determined to leave the house as soon as possible. After entertaining a last party of guests (which included an over-wrought Cosima von Bülow, by then desperately unhappy with her own marriage), Wagner and Minna left the Asyl for the last time on 17 August 1858. They travelled together as far as Zürich railway station and then went their separate ways, she back to Dresden, and he to Venice.

The 'grandeur, beauty and decay' of Venice suited Wagner's melancholy mood and he rented some sparsely furnished rooms in the Palazzo Giustiniani, overlooking the Grand Canal. He was now free of social distractions and at last had the peace and solitude he desired to resume work on *Tristan*. Unfortunately, as well as suffering a spell of bad health, Wagner soon discovered that the legacy of 1848 had followed him even to Italy. Although

Wagner, *c*.1859.

The Palazzo Giustiniani, Venice.

not part of the German Confederation, Venice was still part of the Austrian Empire and therefore came under the jurisdiction of Vienna. The Austrian Chief of Police, Baron Kempen von Fichtenstamm, immediately notified his Foreign Ministry that an undesirable political refugee was residing in Austrian territory; but, despite protestations from the Saxon government, the Ministry recommended only that Wagner be kept under tight police surveillance. The regular reports required by Vienna were written by Angelo Crespi, a local police official, who did an admirable job of putting the authorities' minds at rest, and so gave Wagner the respite he needed to work on *Tristan*.

As he composed, Venice cast its unique spell over Wagner's imagination. From his apartment he could hear the lively bustle of the canal beneath his window; and at night the stillness would be broken only by the mournful song of the gondoliers at they glided past, a sound as ancient and timeless as the city itself. He finished the full score of Act II of *Tristan* on 18 March 1859 and immediately recognised it as 'the highest point of my art so far'. With the threat of a confrontation between Austrian troops and Italian nationalists growing stronger every day, Wagner left Venice on 24 March and travelled to Lucerne. He took a room at the Hotel Schweizerhof, overlooking the lake, and there, on 6 August 1859, he wrote the last bars of the final act of *Tristan* in the presence of the young composer Felix Draeseke.

After two years of hard struggle, *Tristan* was now ready for the world and Wagner was impatient to see his new work performed. Germany and Austria were still out of the question and London was too fresh a painful memory; so, against his better judgement, he decided to make a second serious assault on Paris. On his way there Wagner visited the Wesendoncks in Zürich, with whom, in spite of everything, relations were still cordial (although Mathilde had returned letters unopened that he had written to her from

Venice). Desperate for money, Wagner made a deal with Otto whereby he would buy the copyright of the four *Ring* operas for 6,000 francs each, with Wagner to get the income only from public performances. With the deal signed and sealed and the first instalment in his pocket, in September 1859 Wagner arrived in Paris, where he took a small house in the Rue Newton. Shortly afterwards he was rejoined by Minna, who had been advised by their doctor, Pusinelli, not to resume sexual relations as this would adversely affect her health – a ban on love that Wagner was, in this case, only too happy to comply with.

Since his last visit to Paris in 1850, the number of Wagner's admirers had been growing steadily, due largely to the efforts of a small group of disciples who now helped him gain access into influential artistic circles. Foremost amongst these followers were Auguste de Gasperini, a retired naval surgeon who, after meeting the forty-six-year-old Wagner soon after his arrival in Paris, was struck by 'the severity of his features' which were 'stamped with the iron will that was the basis of his character'. Wagner was still very much a rough-edged provincial Saxon who could never feel at home amid the airs and graces of fashionable Parisian society, and he led a retiring life in the city; although on Wednesday evenings he would throw open his house to a lively company of poets, musicians, artists and scholars, who represented the radical intelligentsia of the day. As always, Wagner dominated these soirées with his irrepressible, manic energy, and would entertain his guests by singing excerpts from his operas.

Wagner's chief ambition in Paris was to see *Tristan* staged, and in order to facilitate its acceptance he organised a series of three concerts of excerpts from his works, held at the Théâtre Italien in January and February 1860. The concerts, attended by such notables as Berlioz, Meyerbeer, Gounod, Champfleury and Baudelaire, were a great success, with every item enthusiastically applauded – apart, that is, from the *Tristan* prelude, which left the vast majority of the audience totally perplexed. Wagner was forced to abandon his idea for a performance of *Tristan* after learning that the concerts had resulted in a deficit of 11,000 francs, which he had no way of repaying; though by a stroke of good fortune, he was able soon afterwards to sell the score of *Das Rheingold* to the music publisher Franz Schott for 10,000 francs. In desperation, he asked Wesendonck to regard the sum *he* had already paid for the opera as an advance payment for the unwritten last part of the *Ring*, an irregular expedient to which his friend good naturedly agreed.

After shelving the *Tristan* plan, Wagner saw his best hope was to get *Tannhäuser* produced at the Opéra. He now had some important friends at court, who took every opportunity to

Princess Pauline Metternich.

Berlioz.

recommend the opera; and at last, on 11 March 1860, a performance of *Tannhäuser* was commanded by Emperor Napoleon III. The person largely responsible for persuading Napoleon to issue his imperial decree was Princess Pauline Metternich, the wife of the Austrian ambassador, who was disliked in certain court circles in Paris for her manly habits and her supposed political mission to bring about a *rapprochement* between France and Austria. Now that *Tannhäuser* was to be performed by order of the emperor – a decision supported by the Austrian, Prussian and even Saxon embassies – the pressure was on King Johann of Saxony to grant at last an amnesty to the errant composer. In July 1860 Johann grudgingly issued a qualified pardon, whereby Wagner was permitted to enter any part of Germany with the exception of Saxony. With mixed emotions, on 12 August he set foot again on German soil for the first time in eleven years.

Staying only a short while in Germany, Wagner returned to Paris for the *Tannhäuser* rehearsals which began at the Opéra on 24 September. There was a rule at the Opéra that all foreign operas had to be performed in French. To comply with this, and also to promote a clearer understanding of his work, Wagner arranged for translations of *Der fliegende Holländer, Tannhäuser, Lohengrin* and *Tristan* to be published together with a long foreword by himself, entitled *Zukunftsmusik* (Music of the Future). However, he refused outright the management's request for the customary second-act ballet, which had long been *de rigueur* at the Opéra to please the aristocratic members of the Jockey Club, who always arrived at the theatre late. As he had long considered the opening scene of *Tannhäuser* to be the weak part of the opera, he willingly compromised by rewriting the Venusberg music and adding a longer and more frenzied Bacchanal. These revisions were completed in January 1861 and, together with the other smaller alterations to the score, constitute the 'Paris' version of *Tannhäuser*.

After no less than 164 rehearsals, during which time Wagner came close to despair with the conductor, Pierre-Louis Dietsch, and his leading singer, Albert Niemann, the first performance of *Tannhäuser* took place on 13 March 1861, with two subsequent performances on 18 and 24 March. The appalling behaviour of a small section of the audience, which succeeded in totally wrecking all three evenings, has gone down as one of the great scandals in theatre history. The young bloods of the Jockey Club, whom Baudelaire described as a 'handful of hooligans', had decided in advance to disrupt the proceedings as a protest against Princess Metternich and the pro-Austrian tendencies of Napoleon's court. Jeering and booing, and blowing on dog whistles, they turned each performance into a fiasco; and after the third night, at Wagner's request, the production was withdrawn. Wagner managed to remain philosophical about the whole affair, realising that he had made many influential and lasting friendships while in Paris. However, he had no money to show from the last eighteen months' work, and had accumulated more debts. He left Paris soon afterwards for Karlsruhe, where he hoped to get *Tristan* performed – the first of the many journeys he was to make over the next three years in his constant quest for artistic recognition and financial stability.

The Grand Duke of Baden was interested in staging the première of *Tristan* in Karlsruhe, and so in April 1861 Wagner went to Vienna to look for suitable soloists. There, he heard *Lohengrin* performed for the first time on 11 May 1861 at the Vienna Court Opera, and in the person of the tenor, Aloys Ander, Wagner believed he had found his Tristan. However, the Opéra

Announcement of the second
Paris performance of
Tannhäuser, 1861.

THEATRE IMPERIAL DE L'OPERA

Les bureaux seront ouverts à 7 heures 1/4.   On commencera à 7 heures 3/4.

57.   Aujourd'hui LUNDI 18 Mars 1861.

DÉBUTS DE M. NIEMANN

DEUXIEME REPRÉSENTATION

TANNHÄUSER

Opéra en TROIS actes et QUATRE tableaux,
De M. RICHARD WAGNER.
Divertissement de M. PETIPA. — Décors de MM. CAMBON, THIERRY, DESPLECHIN, NOLAU et RUBE.

Vénus,
Mme TEDESCO.

Elisabeth,
Mlle MARIE SAX.

Tannhäuser,
M. NIEMANN.

Wolfram,
M. MORELLI.

Hermann,
M. CAZAUX.

Biterolf,
M. COULON.

MM. AIMÈS, KOENIG, FRÉRET, Mlle REBOUX,
Mlles CHRISTIAN, GRANIER, VOGLER, ROUAUD.

DANSE :

Mlles ROUSSEAU, TROISVALLETS, STOIKOFF, ALINE,
MM. LEFÈVRE, MILLOT.

Le Bureau de location, rue Drouot, au coin de la rue Rossini, est ouvert de 10 h. à 6 h.

refused to release him, but instead suggested producing *Tristan* in Vienna; which, in view of the excellent facilities available there, seemed to Wagner a far better prospect than Karlsruhe. He planned to start rehearsals in August, but everything had to be postponed because Ander strained his voice and was unavailable for several months (a misfortune that was used by his enemies, led by the critic Eduard Hanslick, as proof that the opera was unsingable). Depressed, and at a total loose end, in November he unexpectedly received an invitation from the Wesendoncks to join them in Venice. Relations were still friendly, though the couple's renewed affection for each other convinced Wagner of the impossibility of his ever returning to the Asyl. One day, he recounted in *Mein Leben*, the three of them went to see Titian's *Assumption of the Virgin*, and so affected was he by the masterpiece that he decided once again to take up his 'grand comic opera', *Die Meistersinger von Nürnberg*, the sketch of which, written in 1845, was still in Mathilde's possession. In actual fact, he had expressed just such an intention to the publisher Franz Schott only a few weeks previously; though, typically, he neglected to mention this in his autobiography.

Back in Vienna, Wagner wrote a revised prose sketch of *Die Meistersinger* and received an advance of 10,000 francs from Schott's. He then took a room in the Hotel Voltaire in Paris where, in ebullient mood, he wrote the libretto in exactly thirty days, finishing it on 25 January 1862. Anxious to shut out the troubles of the world by immersing himself in the cheerful music of *Die Meistersinger*, Wagner needed another retreat where he could compose in peace and quiet. After giving a public reading of the libretto at Schott's house, he moved into a small house in Biebrich, a village on the Rhine near Mainz, where he was unexpectedly joined a few weeks later by Minna. They talked of setting up home again together, but it was not long before the predictable arguments and recriminations began again and, after 'ten days of hell', Minna returned to Dresden. Shortly afterwards, Wagner applied to King Johann for a full amnesty to allow him access to Saxony on the grounds of Minna's ill health; and this was at last granted, on 28 March 1862.

Minna had made it quite clear that divorce was out of the question, but this did not stop Wagner from enjoying the company of some of his more attractive female admirers. In particular, he was strongly attracted to the twenty-eight-year-old Mathilde Maier, whom he met at a party given by the Schotts. The two soon became firm friends, though the relationship never developed into a full-blown romance. Another young companion he found while at Biebrich was the actress Frederike Meyer, who became a regular guest at his house during the summer of 1862.

Contemporary cartoon of Wagner in Paris.

He reconnoiters.

He appeals to the city's generosity.

Under an amiable inspiration he writes the brochure, *Une Capitulation*.

Consoled by Liszt after the Tannhäuser catastrophe.

Tristan, orchestral sketch for
Act III.

Also at this time he was visited by Ludwig and Malvina Schnorr von Carolsfeld (who were to be the first Tristan and Isolde) and Hans and Cosima von Bülow. Cosima seemed to have lost the shyness and aloofness that Wagner had noted in her on previous meetings and seemed to be full of high spirits, on one occasion consenting to Wagner's suggestion that he push her back to her hotel in a wheelbarrow! The wretched Bülow, who was painfully conscious of being under Wagner's shadow, could only watch helplessly as the blossoming relationship between his idol and his wife pursued its course.

Meanwhile, work on *Die Meistersinger* was progressing slowly, with only the Prelude and some sketches of Acts I and III written. In October 1862 Schott refused Wagner's request for a further advance, which forced him to abandon work on *Die Meistersinger* (the full score of which was not completed until October 1867) and spend the next eighteen months trying to earn a living by giving concerts around Europe. He conducted the first performance of the *Meistersinger* prelude at the Leipzig Gewandhaus on 1 November and then spent a few days with Minna in Dresden, which turned out to be their last meeting.

From there he went to Vienna to conduct three concerts of extracts from the *Ring* and *Die Meistersinger*, which he had arranged himself in Biebrich. With the exception of the *Meistersinger* prelude, all the items in the first concert on 26 December were being heard for the first time, and were a great success with the Viennese audience, the applause being especially tumultuous after the 'Ride of the Valkyries'. The pattern was repeated for the other two concerts on 1 and 11 January 1863, and the series ended to popular acclaim, the usual bad reviews and an inevitable deficit.

At the end of 1862 Wagner wrote a preface to the first edition of the *Ring* poem to go on sale to the public, in which he outlined once again his ideas for a festival theatre where his operas could be performed in ideal conditions. A German prince would be the most likely person to fund such a venture, he wrote. 'Is such a prince to be found?' After the financial disappointment of Vienna, however, Wagner could not afford to sit back and wait for a royal patron to appear. In February 1863 he went on to Prague to give another concert and this was followed by eight concerts in St Petersburg and Moscow, from which he actually came home with a profit. In May, Wagner moved into the upper storey of a house in Penzing, near Vienna, and soon disposed of his hard-earned Russian money by spending extravagantly on luxurious decorations and furnishings for his new flat. The rest of the year was punctuated by conducting engagements and a desperate search for funds, which culminated, in true Wagnerian style, in a lavish Christmas celebration at Penzing. With reckless abandon he put up a huge tree and showered his friends with what was, according to his companion Peter Cornelius, 'a king's ransom in gifts'.

By March 1864 Wagner's financial situation had become hopeless and he was advised by a legal friend to leave for Switzerland without delay to avoid arrest for debt. Passing through Munich he spotted in a shop window a portrait of the eighteen-year-old King Ludwig II, who on 10 March had succeeded his father Maximilian II on the throne of Bavaria. Wagner immediately felt sympathy for the young man, who at such a tender age had been placed in an extremely difficult position. Arriving in Zürich, Wagner sought refuge with the Willes, as the Wesendoncks had refused to accommodate him. At

Act III, Scene 5 of *Die Meistersinger*.

their house in Mariafeld, he one day launched into the famous outburst to Eliza Wille in which he expressed his defiance against the world:

I am a different kind of organism, my nerves are hypersensitive – I must have beauty, splendour and light! The world owes me what I need! I cannot live the miserable life of a town organist like your master Bach! Is it so shocking, if I think I deserve the little bit of luxury I like? I, who have so much enjoyment to give the world and thousands of people?'‡

After a month, relations with the Willes were becoming strained and Wagner left Mariafeld on 29 April for Stuttgart, where he hoped to recommence work on *Die Meistersinger*. He was joined there by his friend Wendelin Weissheimer, who found him in a near-suicidal state of mind. The two of them decided to search for a peaceful haven for Wagner, somewhere in the country; but the evening before he was due to leave Stuttgart, he received a message that a gentleman from Munich wished to speak to him on a matter of some urgency. Assuming that he was one of his more determined creditors, Wagner refused to see him until the following morning, when the stranger introduced himself as Franz von Pfistermeister, Cabinet Secretary to the King of

‡ Translated by Mary Whittall, reproduced from Curt von Westernhagen, *Wagner: A Biography*.

86

Bavaria. He presented Wagner with a ring and a photograph of the King and told him that Ludwig had always been a fervent admirer of his work and wished to help him out of his difficulties. As the King, above all, wished to meet the poet and composer of *Lohengrin*, Pfistermeister (who had been on Wagner's trail for weeks) proposed they leave for Munich immediately; and on 4 May 1864, in the Munich Residenz, Wagner stood for the first time before his new royal benefactor.

Wagner, *c*.1863.

9 Ludwig

King Ludwig II of Bavaria.

Ludwig II ascended to the throne of Bavaria on 10 March 1864, after the sudden death of his father, Maximilian II. The young king was only eighteen and had no real knowledge of the practice of government, or of the responsibilities involved in ruling over the richest and most powerful state in southern Germany. As well as this, Ludwig was a highly strung and rather morbidly romantic youth who far preferred the solitude of the Bavarian forests and lakes to the pomp and ceremony usually associated with monarchy, and he actively avoided exposing himself to the gaze of the Munich crowds. Despite his aloofness, his subjects were much taken by their new King, whose eccentricity and almost feminine grace and beauty made a welcome change after nearly twenty years of Maximilian's pragmatic and charmless rule.

Ludwig spent most of his childhood in the ancient castle of Hohenschwangau, the Royal Family's country home, which has since been overshadowed by his later building follies – the bizarre castles of Neuschwanstein, Herrenchiemsee and Linderhof, which Ludwig built, at great expense, high in the Bavarian mountains. Maximilian had decorated the walls of Hohenschwangau with pictures of the Swan Knight, an ancient German legend that greatly appealed to Ludwig's extravagant romanticism. Locked away in his private dream world amidst the solitude of the trees and mountains, Ludwig came to see the swan as the idealisation of all his romantic yearnings; and just as they adorned the grounds of the castle, so the swans filled the melancholy landscape of the young prince's imagination. When, at the age of fifteen, he saw a performance of *Lohengrin* (in which the Knight of the Grail magically appears in a boat drawn by a swan) he was deeply affected by Wagner's music and his dramatic treatment of the *Lohengrin* legend, and Ludwig believed he had at last found an artist whose romantic vision was in perfect accord with his own. With growing fascination, he immersed himself in Wagner's essays and when he read the preface to the new edition of the *Ring* poem, which ended with the question 'Is such a prince to be found?', he became fully convinced of the path along which his duty and his destiny lay.

The friendship between Ludwig and Wagner lasted, despite various troubled periods, until the composer's death. The fact that they were able to overcome some seemingly irreconcilable personal differences along the way is evidence that their friendship existed very largely on a higher, theatrical plane, as is clear from the tone of their voluminous correspondence. Ludwig's letter to Wagner the day after their first meeting contained the sort of high-flown and heavily stylised language that was to remain at the heart of their relationship:

Stylisation of Ludwig II as the Swan Knight.

I want to lift the menial burdens of everyday life from your shoulders for ever. I want to enable you to enjoy the peace for which you so long, so that you will be able to unfurl the mighty pinions of your genius unhindered in the pure ether of your rapturous art! Unknowingly you were the sole source of my joys from my earliest boyhood, my friend who spoke to my heart as no other could, my best mentor and teacher.‡

Ludwig's professed understanding of Wagner's artistic mission and his promise to give him every assistance in completing and staging the *Ring*, drew from Wagner similar expressions of rapture and heartfelt gratitude. In letters to his friends, he described their initial meeting as a 'love scene', in which Ludwig, his saviour, 'so handsome and glorious, so great in soul', who loved him with 'all the passion of a first love', had offered to satisfy all his earthly needs, with no conditions attached – 'no appointment, no duties, I need only be his friend.' The ecstatic language of their correspondence has given rise to speculation as to whether there was any homosexual attachment between Wagner and Ludwig, although no tangible evidence exists to support this case. Ludwig's homosexuality is well documented, but Wagner never showed any tendencies in this direction. Indeed, any intrusion of sexual feelings into the relationship would never have been countenanced by the King, whose conception of Wagner, and of art, was always heavily idealised.

This is not to say, however, that Ludwig was blind to the faults of Wagner the man. Although he remained faithful to Wagner's artistic vision and gave and lent him a vast sum of money over the years, he at times showed considerable exasperation at Wagner's lack of probity in financial and personal matters, and was saddened to discover on several occasions Wagner's capacity for destructiveness and duplicity. Ludwig preferred to see Wagner as the composer of *Lohengrin*, the creator of a magical world about which he used to daydream. He shared Wagner's belief in the supreme importance of art in human affairs and considered it to be their joint mission to regenerate German culture in order that future centuries would be better able to understand the higher glories of Wagnerian music drama. Wagner himself was never entirely happy with the arrangement whereby he was completely dependent on royal patronage for the realisation of his ideas; but, despite his frequent annoyance at Ludwig's interference in artistic matters, he had no wish to return to the hardships he had so recently put behind him and was prudent enough not to risk a rift by openly challenging the King. He was also genuinely grateful to his benefactor for so generously giving him the means to complete

‡ Translated by Mary Whittall, reproduced from Curt von Westernhagen, *Wagner: A Biography*.

90

Schloss Berg on Lake
Starnberg.

his life's work; and although he sometimes abused Ludwig's trust,
he was largely undeserving of the obloquy heaped upon him by his
Ministers and advisers, who were to take every opportunity to
denounce Wagner as a sybarite and a schemer, exploiting his
position as the King's favourite to further his own political
ambitions.

Following their first meeting on 4 May 1864, Wagner was given
4,000 gulden by Ludwig to settle the most pressing of his Viennese
debts, followed by a further 16,000 gulden in June. Ludwig also
lent him a house, the Villa Pellet on Lake Starnberg, just a short
drive from the royal castle Schloss Berg where Wagner and his
'pupil' would meet every day to discuss their plans for the future.
This period of heady wonderment lasted for a month or so, after
which Wagner began to grow more conscious of his essential
isolation and lonely bachelor existence, and his thoughts turned
once again to seeking a female companion. He appealed to
Mathilde Maier to come and 'keep house' for him, but she refused,
despite Wagner's expedient of writing to her mother assuring her

91

of his strictly honourable intentions. However, his disappointment was soon forgotten, for on 29 June, Cosima von Bülow arrived unexpectedly at the Villa Pellet, accompanied by her two young daughters, Daniella and Blandine. It seems likely that up until this time, no word of love had been spoken between Wagner and Cosima (even though a passage in *Mein Leben* claims they vowed to 'belong only to each other' as early as November 1863); but during the week Cosima was at Starnberg before her husband arrived, their true feelings were openly expressed and the relationship consummated. Wagner's first child, Isolde, was born on 10 April 1865, the same day that Bülow conducted the first orchestral rehearsal of *Tristan*.

In a letter written to Mathilde Maier in January 1863, Wagner said that he needed 'a woman with the resolution to devote herself to me', who 'would abandon all human relationships which could serve no purpose in the life and work of such a man as myself'. Throughout his life he always felt the need for feminine society and would eagerly form attachments with those women who were unquestioningly responsive to his personality and his art. However, his relationships with Jessie Laussot, Mathilde Maier and Mathilde Wesendonck, although all serving some aspect of his romantic and idealised notion of what a woman's role should be, ultimately failed to provide him with the intellectual (and sexual) stimulation he came to require in his later years. Wagner came to realise that the submissive, self-sacrificing ideal of feminine virtue he personified in many of his operatic heroines could not alone, when translated into human terms, fulfil his basic desire for simple domestic contentment with an intelligent companion, who could complement his creative genius by giving him practical assistance, understanding and reassurance. In Cosima he found such a companion and although there was never any question of 'equality' in the relationship (Wagner was too domineering, and Cosima too awestruck for this ever to have been the case), it provided him with the emotional and sexual stability he needed in the last fifteen years of his life.

Although certainly acquiescent to her 'Master' in most respects, Cosima was in many ways a remarkable woman in her own right, as she was to show in her efficient running of the Bayreuth festival after Wagner's death, working tirelessly to establish it as an international event until she handed over the reins to her son Siegfried in 1906 (she died in April 1930, at the age of ninety-two). Cosima was one of three illegitimate children of Liszt and the Countess Marie d'Agoult, who were lovers for five years before Liszt met Princess Caroline Wittgenstein. The children were brought up in Paris under the strict tutelage of the Princess's former Russian governess, who gave her young charges an

Bülow conducting *Tristan*.

Hans von Bülow.

education in keeping with their aristocratic breeding; the subjects ranging equally from music and modern languages to deportment and other social graces. Cosima emerged from her formative years with a seriousness of mind and strength of character that were to prepare her for her chosen role as the helper and protector of genius.

Cosima's erudition, her thirst for knowledge, her love of reading, her practical abilities and, above all, her desire to serve him completely, made her an ideal companion for Wagner. Yet behind her accomplished and cultivated Parisian exterior she was troubled by doubts, insecurities and prejudices, which earlier had influenced her decision to enter into a disastrous first marriage with Hans von Bülow – a marriage that was, due to Bülow's weakness and chronic inferiority complex, doomed from the start. (Later she was, unwittingly, to help establish an evil legacy at Bayreuth by foolishly championing Wagner's racial theories, the repercussions of which still linger, in many people's minds, to this day.) Cosima's total devotion to Wagner and to his artistic mission is borne out by entries in her famous Diaries, which she began in 1869 and continued to keep until Wagner's death. Surprisingly, very few of Cosima's own opinions and feelings can be gleaned from these pages; for so completely was her personality subsumed into his that sometimes it is almost impossible to tell just whose views are being expressed, especially as Cosima would always refrain from expressing any opinion on artistic matters that did not accord with Wagner's. She had, she said, 'only one wish, to serve!', and the Diaries frequently sink to embarrassing depths of servility and hero-worship, hitting rock bottom in an entry from July 1878, when Cosima recorded that one morning she had been graced with the gift of a few hairs from Wagner's eyebrows! The fact remains, however, that Cosima was the only woman Wagner ever consulted about the composition of his operas (albeit rarely), and by her subtle powers of persuasion she was able to exercise control over events and influence the course of his life in many other significant ways.

By the time Bülow arrived in Starnberg on 7 July 1864, the fate of music's most famous *ménage à trois* had already been sealed. It is not known for certain when he became fully aware of the nature of the relationship between his wife and Wagner, but it is possible that he was informed sometime during his short stay at the Villa Pellet. Bülow had always been convinced of his unworthiness of Cosima and had sworn to Liszt in the early days of their courtship that he would not hesitate to 'release her should she become aware that she has been deceived in me'; so with such an attitude it is likely that he was able to accept without too much agonising Cosima's decision to link her destiny with a man he also worshipped. Like his wife, Bülow felt it was his duty to assist Wagner in his artistic mission, and was prepared to go along with the subsequent conspiracy of silence to prevent news of the affair from reaching Ludwig who, they believed (with good reason, as it turned out) would react with hostility to such a scandal.

After a few weeks in Starnberg, the three split up, Wagner not seeing Cosima again on a regular basis until the Bülow family took up permanent residence in Munich in November 1864. Ludwig had been away on official business for most of June and July and so had, unwittingly, given them the freedom to seal their relationship. On the King's return, Wagner presented him with an essay, 'On the State and Religion', a lofty tract exalting the role of monarchy in constitutional affairs, following this tribute with

Cosima in the first years of her marriage to Bülow.

Ludwig II, photograph presented to Wagner by the king.

the *Huldigungsmarsch* (Homage March), composed for Ludwig's nineteenth birthday on 25 August. On 26 September 1864 Wagner informed the King that he had resolved to put all other work aside in order to complete 'my major work, the *Ring*'. The next day he took up *Siegfried* once again, making a fair copy of the score of Act I, and (in December) starting on the scoring of Act II, which he finished on 2 December 1865.

In October 1864 Wagner moved into a spacious new house at 21 Briennerstrasse in Munich, which Ludwig had generously made available to him. Just as he had done at Penzing the previous year, he spent lavishly on luxurious furnishings, exotic scents and expensive silk clothes for his wardrobe, decking out the whole house in the most sumptuous fabrics his milliner in Vienna could supply. Wagner insisted, as always, that he needed such opulence to stimulate his senses and aid his creativity, but the growing number of his enemies at court saw it merely as a sign of his wanton extravagance and decadence, and along with the local

Cartoon of the relationship between Wagner, Cosima and Bülow.

press were to make much capital out of Wagner's eccentric lifestyle in order to influence public opinion against him.

Further eyebrows were raised when, on 18 October, Ludwig formally granted Wagner the financial means to complete the *Ring* by having a contract drawn up with the Royal Treasury, giving the King the ownership of the copyright for the not inconsiderable sum of 30,000 gulden (so making him the third purchaser, the first being Wesendonck). From 1864 onwards, Ludwig gave Wagner a total of over half-a-million marks, not counting his magnanimous support of the Bayreuth festival scheme with a sum not far short of this amount (this money was later repaid by Wagner's heirs); but because the King had no private fortune, his patronage of Wagner had to be financed from the Civil List. This inevitably caused indignation amongst Ludwig's Cabinet officials, who saw Wagner as a dangerous adventurer who was exerting a pernicious influence over their King for his own ends. During the next year, the anti-Wagner faction never missed an opportunity to pillory him in the newspapers and attempt to discredit him in the eyes of the King, and after a concerted and vicious campaign they finally succeeded in hounding him out of Bavaria altogether by the end of 1865.

Gottfried Semper.

The Residenz and (right) the Court Theatre, where *Tristan* was premièred.

After the signing of the contract, Ludwig was impatient to see the *Ring* performed, and at his prompting Wagner sent for his architect friend Gottfried Semper and asked him to design a suitable theatre in Munich. The plan immediately came up against a wall of hostility from Ludwig's Ministers and, in the end, the theatre was never built, although Wagner was to incorporate many of its projected features – such as the sunken orchestra pit – into the Bayreuth Festspielhaus. Another ill-fated scheme was Wagner's proposed Music School, which he envisaged as a training ground for singers in a new German style of singing that was suited to the needs of Wagnerian music drama. As with the theatre project, Ludwig's Ministers again thwarted Wagner's plan, even though it undoubtedly had the King's support.

The most implacable of Wagner's enemies at court was Ludwig von der Pfordten, Ludwig's new Chief Minister, who had encountered Wagner before in Saxony in 1848, when he had been minister of Culture under Friedrich August II. At the time, Pfordten had strongly disapproved of Wagner's revolutionary activities and since then had followed his career with growing resentment. He regarded Wagner and his music with undisguised loathing and was horrified that this Protestant revolutionary (Bavaria was strongly Catholic) should be allowed to exert such an influence over Ludwig. Added to this, Bülow's appointment as *Vorspieler* to the King, a post that Wagner had secured for him, had signalled the arrival in Munich of more and more of Wagner's

97

entourage who, it was felt, behaved with unbearable arrogance towards their Bavarian hosts.

The plan for a festival theatre was the final straw for Pfordten and the anti-Wagner faction and, in February 1865, they made their first attempt to discredit Wagner with the King. Cabinet Secretary Pfistermeister reported to Ludwig that Wagner had not only misled him over a payment for a portrait, but also had disrespectfully referred to the King as *Mein Junge* (my boy). In a fit of pique, Ludwig refused to see Wagner when he arrived for an audience on 6 February and, although the misunderstanding was patched up within a few days, it gave the press the opportunity to question Wagner's probity and attack him for the extravagance of his lifestyle at 21 Briennerstrasse. Wagner drew from Ludwig an assurance that 'everything will be as wonderful as it used to be', and with the King's trust confirmed he was able to concentrate on the pressing matter of preparations for the première of *Tristan*, scheduled to take place at the Munich Hoftheater on 15 May. Bülow was to conduct, and Wagner had managed to secure the services of Ludwig Schnorr von Carolsfeld and his wife Malvina to sing the lead roles. When the big day arrived, however, it brought with it a double disaster: in the morning, the bailiffs turned up on Wagner's doorstep in connection with an old Paris debt, and in the afternoon he was informed that Malvina had lost her voice and would not be able to sing Isolde. There was no choice but to

Designs for Tristan and Isolde's costumes.

Ludwig and Malvina Schnorr von Carolsfeld.

postpone the performance, to the manifest delight of those who maintained that the opera was unsingable and unperformable.

The première of *Tristan* eventually took place, to a full house, on 10 June 1865, followed by three subsequent performances over the next month. The evening was a great success. Schnorr was superb as Tristan, Ludwig trembled with ecstasy in the royal box and, despite the usual hostility of most of the critics, many of the audience realised that they had just witnessed an epoch-making event in the history of music. Tragically, three weeks after the final performance Schnorr died suddenly in Dresden, possibly of typhus, though a legend quickly sprang up that the superhuman demands of the role had caused his death. Three years later Wagner attempted to quash this rumour in a published essay entitled *My Recollections of Ludwig Schnorr von Carolsfeld*, but the real cause of the singer's death remains a mystery to this day.

Design for the première of *Tristan*.

At Ludwig's request, on 17 July 1865 Wagner began the dictation of his autobiography *Mein Leben* to Cosima, who was by this time an almost permanent fixture at 21 Briennerstrasse. She was his secretary, housekeeper and mistress all rolled into one, and she began to exert her influence on everything from his manners to his choice of friends. During periods of enforced absence from each other, she encouraged Wagner to record for her all his heartfelt thoughts in a notebook known as the 'Brown Book', which he continued to do until 1868. Another aspect of Cosima's character, her aristocratic *sang-froid*, was put to the test in October 1865, after Wagner had once again negotiated successfully with the King for more money. In an atmosphere of mounting hostility at court, the Cabinet had agreed, at Ludwig's insistence, to grant Wagner an annual payment of 8,000 gulden plus a lump sum of 40,000 gulden, which he was invited to collect from the Treasury. As Wagner was ill at the time, Cosima went instead to pick up the money, but when she arrived she was given not banknotes but sacks full of silver coins to take away. Finding herself on the receiving end of this deliberate ploy to embarrass the Master, Cosima, in fine style, coolly went and found two cabs and loaded the sacks into them herself. This story quickly spread around Munich and added fuel to the growing speculation regarding the true nature of Wagner's relationship with Cosima.

After the thwarting of his plans for a festival theatre and music school, it became clear to Wagner that his enemies were trying to wear him down, and that if he were to win this war of attrition he must use his influence over Ludwig to consolidate his position. During the latter part of 1865 Wagner became increasingly drawn, albeit reluctantly, into affairs of state – an expedient that gave Ludwig's Ministers the excuse to force the King's hand and have him expelled from Munich. Aware that Wagner had started to 'advise' Ludwig on Cabinet matters, Pfistermeister, Pfordten and their colleagues, now feeling their positions to be genuinely threatened, cunningly drew from Wagner a public admission of his meddling in Bavarian politics. On 26 November 1865 the Munich *Volksbote* carried a scathing attack on Wagner, to which he responded three days later with an anonymous letter – whose authorship was nevertheless obvious – in the *Neueste Nachrichten* calling for the 'removal of two or three individuals' from the Cabinet. This was the indiscretion that his enemies had been waiting for, and Pfordten quickly wrote to the King demanding that he choose between 'the love and respect of your faithful subjects and the friendship of Richard Wagner'. Ludwig's first instinct was to defend his friend, but the knives were now drawn and, under enormous pressure from his Ministers, the Church and the aristocracy, who warned him of possible mass resignations – and even revolution – the King reluctantly gave the order for Wagner's expulsion. Early on the morning of 10 December 1865, a pale and distraught Wagner said goodbye to Cosima and his friends at Munich station and departed Bavaria; en route, once again, for Switzerland.

Arriving in Geneva in early January 1866, Wagner took a house (Les Artichauts) just outside the town where he resumed work on Act I of *Die Meistersinger*, completing the full score of the act on 23 March. He bore no grudge against Ludwig, but rather tried to impress upon him, in a letter, that the King had been forced into making his decision as a result of the lies and trickery of Pfistermeister and Pfordten who, he urged, should be summarily dismissed – advice that Ludwig felt unable to follow. However, despite his temporary banishment, Wagner's income from the Royal Treasury seemed assured, and soon after moving into Les Artichauts be began to look around for a suitable permanent residence in the south of France. While in Marseilles for a few days at the end of January, Wagner unexpectedly received a telegram

from Dr Pusinelli telling him that Minna had died suddenly in Dresden. The news grieved him deeply, and although he did not feel up to travelling to Dresden to pay his last respects he would, in the future, recall her memory with some fondness, despite the bitterness of their years together.

Unsuccessful in his house-hunting, Wagner settled down at Les Artichauts with *Die Meistersinger*. Cosima arrived on 8 March and stayed for the rest of the month. Before she returned to Munich the two of them travelled to Lake Lucerne in the hope of finding a suitable home where they could eventually settle down together, and there they spotted a large and attractive house on a promontory overlooking the lake, called Tribschen. Within a few days Wagner had taken a year's lease on the house, and on 15 April 1866 he moved into Tribschen, where he was to spend the next six years of his life. On 15 May, soon after he had been joined once again by Cosima, Wagner received a shock telegram from Ludwig announcing his intention to abdicate, a course of action that would have had a disastrous effect on Wagner's fortune. He managed to dissuade him, though the King remained deeply depressed, partly due to his enforced absence from Wagner, but largely because of his worries over the worsening political situation in Germany.

Otto von Bismarck, the Prussian Prime Minister, was determined to establish Prussian hegemony in Germany and undermine Austrian dominance there. Bismarck considered that Prussia, now the most powerful state both economically and militarily, was hampered in its ambitions by the creaking German Confederation presided over by Austria, who, together with the smaller German states, could always outvote Prussia, so giving a

Tribschen on Lake Lucerne.

false picture of the true distribution of power. At stake was the leadership of the emerging German national state, and Bismarck realised that if a Hohenzollern emperor was to rule the second German *Reich* (1871-1918) then the question of Austrian versus Prussian rivalry must be decided, in time-honoured fashion, on the battlefield . As the stormclouds gathered in the early months of 1866, it became clear that the German governments must choose which side they were to support. Deeply mistrustful of Bismarck the vast majority of them, including Bavaria and Saxony, supported Austria, though even their combined efforts were to no avail. The Austro-Prussian war broke out on 14 June 1866, with the well-drilled Prussian war machine proving more than a match for the outdated forces of the Confederation. Following victories

Otto von Bismarck with Napoleon III on the left.

over the Austrians at Königgrätz and the Bavarians at Kissingen (10 July), Bismarck formed the new North German Confederation under the presidency of King Wilhelm I of Prussia, who was later to wear the imperial crown of the German Empire, with Bismarck as chancellor.

During the build-up to war, Wagner freely gave advice to Ludwig on the Prussian question (the King even visited him personally at Tribschen on 22 May, to the fury of his Ministers) but, in common with many German liberals and intellectuals, his attitude towards Bismarck was equivocal. Although inspired by the idea of a united Germany, Wagner had earlier regarded Bismarck as an arrogant, 'ambitious Junker'; though his view seemed to change after the outbreak of war, and he wrote to Röckel urging him to 'stick fast to Bismarck and Prussia'. As it turned out, apart from some financial indemnities, Bavaria was not made to suffer by Bismarck after the battle of Kissingen and, somewhat surprisingly, Ludwig's stature among his subjects seemed to increase. One happy result of the war for Wagner was the resignation at the end of 1866 of his two arch-enemies, Pfistermeister and Pfordten, who had both been vociferous supporters of the Austrian camp, although their removal did not alter his decision never again to settle in Munich.

In June 1866, as war loomed, other stormclouds were gathering at Tribschen. Bülow, who by this time was under no illusions as to the true nature of the relationship between Wagner and his wife, resigned as *Vorspieler* to the King in protest at the relentless, innuendo-filled press campaign being waged against the three of them. He was particularly incensed by a reference in the Munich *Volksbote* to Cosima being 'with her "friend" (or what?) in Lucerne', and even challenged the editor to a duel. Wagner quickly drafted a letter for Ludwig to sign, vindicating Bülow's honour and deploring the way they had all been treated, and Cosima added her own plea to the King. Although by this time suspicious himself, Ludwig once again consented to Wagner's request, and Bülow duly published the letter. The outbreak of war temporarily took the heat off the affair, but it resurfaced again in November when Ludwig Schnorr's widow, Malvina, arrived at Tribschen, in a distraught state. She had, she said, been in touch with the spirit of her dead husband, who had told her that her destiny lay at Wagner's side – a ghostly command that Wagner scornfully rejected, causing the furious Malvina to denounce the adulterous pair to the King. Once again, Wagner and Cosima had to resort to subterfuge (with more than a little malice towards Malvina) to save themselves from exposure. Wagner believed that lying was one of the worst sins, yet felt that it was necessary to protect his precious friendship with Ludwig, on whom so many of

105

Cosima's children: Isolde and Blandine (standing), Eva, Siegfried and Daniela.

his artistic schemes depended. Similarly, Bülow, although the cuckold in the affair, had no wish to upset public opinion, or that of his father-in-law (now the Abbé Liszt), and for the sake of appearances was willing to keep up the charade.

Wagner finished the orchestral sketch of Act II of *Die Meistersinger* on 23 September 1866 and began the composition sketch of Act III the following month. Early the next year, on 22 January 1867, Ludwig announced his engagement to his cousin, Princess Sophie (which he broke off in October), and on 17 February Cosima gave birth to Wagner's second child, Eva. Everything at this time seemed to be going smoothly. Semper was encouraged to proceed with his plans for a festival theatre, Bülow was made *Kapellmeister* by royal decree, and Hans Richter, the future conducter of the *Ring*, joined the household at Tribschen as Wagner's secretary and assistant. However, it became gradually apparent that Ludwig's enthusiasm to discuss Wagner's various artistic schemes was not matched by a determination to put them into practice. Also, the removal of Pfistermeister and Pfordten did not by any means signal the end of official opposition in Munich to Wagner and his circle, and one by one his cherished plans were again shelved. Eventually, Semper became so exasperated by the constant procrastination over the building of the festival theatre that in March 1868 he took recourse to legal action to secure payment for the work he had already done on the plans and models, so signalling the end of yet another ambitious project and further convincing Wagner that Munich was clearly not the place to produce the *Ring*.

In an atmosphere of cosy domesticity at Tribschen, surrounded by his friends and his menagerie of animals and birds, Wagner spent the better part of 1867 working on the final act of *Die Meistersinger*, which he completed on 24 October. The première, on 21 June 1868 at the Court Theatre in Munich, was a huge success. At the King's request, Wagner acknowledged the applause from the royal box itself – a serious breach of etiquette that was widely criticised in the papers the next day. Within a few years *Die Meistersinger* had established itself all over Germany as the supreme festival opera for all manner of patriotic occasions, and was hailed not only as a landmark in the development of truly German art, but as a reflection of the rising tide of German nationalism that gripped the country up to and following unification in 1871.

Wagner at Tribschen, 1868.

Hans Sachs's famous (and controversial) call to the people at the end of *Die Meistersinger* to honour the traditions of their masters and so preserve 'Holy German art', even in the event of foreign domination, was intended primarily by Wagner as a paean to German culture and the German spirit rather than as a chauvinistic declaration of German superiority. Whatever Wagner's artistic intentions, however, Sachs's speech perfectly captured the nationalistic mood of the era, especially that of the rising middle classes; and after Hitler and the Nazis had adopted the opera and re-interpreted Sachs's words in a more sinister light, the continuing notoriety of *Die Meistersinger* was guaranteed. It is also clear from his writings at this time that Wagner's once progressive politics were becoming increasingly reactionary, if not chauvinistic – a fact that did not escape the notice of his old revolutionary acquaintance Heinrich Laube who, to Wagner's great annoyance, published an article in a Vienna newspaper attacking what he perceptively saw as Wagner's revisionist political tendencies emerging in *Die Meistersinger*.

On 16 November 1868 Cosima took the decisive step and moved into Tribschen with her daughters Isolde and Eva; and on 1 January

Friedrich Nietzsche.

Act I Scene I of *Die Meistersinger*.

1869 made the first entry in the diary that she continued to keep until the end of Wagner's life. Bülow still insisted on keeping up appearances to the world at large, though Ludwig had to be officially informed, and this latest turn of events put further strain on the already uneasy relations between Wagner and the King. For Wagner however, Cosima's arrival, and the much-needed emotional stability she brought into his life, proved invaluable aids to his creativity; and after a few months of settling in to family life, he once again took up the task of composing the *Ring*, after a break of twelve years. The composition sketch of the third act of *Siegfried* was begun on 1 March 1869 and completed on 14 June. The full score was completed on 5 February 1871, by which time Wagner was seriously considering Bayreuth rather than Munich as the site for his projected music festival.

Shortly after starting work on *Siegfried*, Wagner had as a guest at Tribschen the twenty-four-year-old philosopher Friedrich Nietzsche, whom he had met the previous year in Leipzig. This

Above:
Judith Gautier

Above right:
Costume designs for Eva and
Stolzing (*Die Meistersinger*,
1868).

visit to Tribschen in May 1869 was the first of many visits
Nietzsche made to the house, and he soon came to be regarded by
Wagner and Cosima as a loyal disciple and an able collaborator.
Himself a talented pianist, Nietzsche – who in 1869 had just been
appointed Professor of Classical Philology at Basle University –
was a passionate admirer of Wagner's music, especially *Tristan*,
and dedicated to Wagner his first major published work, *The Birth
of Tragedy from the Spirit of Music* (1872), in which he argued that
Wagnerian opera was a natural successor to Greek drama. The
friendship between the two men continued unabated until 1876,
when a rift occurred, for reasons that are not entirely clear.
Nietzsche's objections to certain aspects of the first Bayreuth
festival and his disgust at Wagner's apparent surrender to
Christianity with *Parsifal* contributed to the break, though more
importantly Nietzsche had come to believe that his own
intellectual development would be best served by removing
himself from Wagner's sphere of influence.

Nietzsche was still a guest at Tribschen when Wagner's third
child, Siegfried, was born on 6 June 1869, eight days before the
composition of *Siegfried* was completed. 'Only now has our child
been born', declared Cosima upon seeing the finished manuscript.
This happy summer at Tribschen continued with the arrival of
more congenial company in the statuesque form of Judith Gautier,
the attractive and intelligent daughter of the poet Théophile
Gautier, together with her husband and the poet Villiers de l'Isle
Adam. All were devoted admirers, and Wagner was immediately
taken by Judith's charms – not least her physical ones – although
their celebrated 'love affair' did not begin until after the first

Bayreuth festival in 1876, when Wagner was in the thick of composing *Parsifal*.

In the autumn of 1869 a confrontation between Ludwig and Wagner seemed imminent. Wagner was convinced that the *Ring* could not be performed satisfactorily in a conventional theatre, so that Ludwig's expressed intention to see *Das Rheingold* premièred in Munich filled him with dismay – the more so as he had developed an especial loathing for Munich due to the treatment he had received there. Ignoring Wagner's protestations, however, the King was determined to proceed, and rehearsals began in August. It was clear from the start that there were woeful technical inadequacies and, to lend weight to Wagner's objections, the conductor Hans Richter withdrew – a move which infuriated Ludwig, who accused Wagner and his 'theatre rabble' of hatching criminal intrigues to prevent the première taking place. In the end, a local conductor, Franz Wüllner, took up the baton, and *Das Rheingold* received its first performance on 22 September 1869. The following year, once more at Ludwig's insistence and against Wagner's wishes, the première of *Die Walküre* took place in Munich on 26 June 1870, with Wüllner again conducting.

110

Act III of *Die Walküre*. The Valkyries flee as Wotan approaches.

Above left:
Final scene of *Das Rheingold*. A rainbow bridge leads to Valhalla.

Below left:
Announcement of première of *Das Rheingold*.

With the *Rheingold* experience still fresh in his mind, and with work under way on the composition sketch of Act I of *Götterdämmerung* – the final opera in the *Ring* cycle – Wagner started to give serious consideration to finding a suitable venue for the first *Ring* festival. The small Franconian town of Bayreuth had, he remembered, made a pleasing impression on him the one time he had passed through there en route to Prague in 1835, and in March 1870 he looked it up in the encyclopaedia, discovering to his delight that it possessed a theatre – the Markgräfliches Opernhaus – whose unusually large stage made it a possible candidate for staging the *Ring*. Wagner was also against holding the festival in a large city, and was attracted by Bayreuth's pleasant provinciality. Added to this was the town's geographical position halfway between Munich and Berlin, a feature which Wagner thought would be significant should an alliance between Bavaria and Prussia ever become a reality.

The Bayreuth plan quickly took hold of Wagner's imagination, though no sooner had he begun some research into the town than external events intervened to turn his thoughts temporarily in other directions. Bismarck was anxious to precipitate the

111

View of Bayreuth from the
Festival Theatre.

Caricature referring to
Napoleon III's defeat at
Sedan.

L'AIGLE DEPLUMÉ.

formation of a unified Germany, and considered that the best way
to arouse national German public opinon, and bring the southern
states into line, was a war against the old enemy France. Forced
into a corner by Bismarck's deliberately provocative proposals to
put a Hohenzollern prince on the throne of Spain, France duly
declared war on 19 July 1870, the day after Wagner heard that
Cosima's marriage to Bülow had been legally dissolved in Berlin.

Bavaria, along with the other southern states, sided with
Prussia, and the whole of Germany suddenly found an outlet for
its pent-up national pride in the heady excitement of battle. As the
formidable Prussian army stormed through France, Wagner and
Cosima were married in the Protestant church in Lucerne on
25 August. A week later the French were decisively defeated at
Sedan and Napoleon III was deposed, marking the end of the
Second Empire and the formation of the Third Republic.
Resistance continued, but France eventually capitulated after
Paris was besieged during the winter of 1870-71 and reduced
almost to starvation. In January 1871 the new German Empire was
proclaimed in the Hall of Mirrors at Versailles and, at the behest of
the other German states, Wilhelm I of Prussia accepted the
imperial crown, and became Kaiser.

The Franco-Prussian war aroused strong feelings in Germany,
not least at Tribschen, where Wagner gave full vent to his long-
held hatred of the French. In November 1870 he wrote a farcical

Caricature of Wagner on the cover of *L'Eclipse*, a Paris weekly.

Proclamation of the German Empire at Versailles, 1871.

play, entitled *A Capitulation*, in which he mocked the beleaguered Parisians, as well as attacking those Germans who abandoned their culture in favour of the frivolity of French opera. In complete contrast, Wagner's essay *Beethoven*, which upheld Schopenhauer's elevation of music, was published at the end of 1870; and on Christmas morning that year Cosima received her unique 'symphonic birthday greeting', the *Siegfried Idyll*, composed and secretly rehearsed that autumn, and played for her by a small band of fifteen musicians positioned on the stairs outside her room.

After the coronation of Wilhelm I (which Wagner celebrated by writing a concert piece, the *Kaisermarsch*), events in Europe settled down and Wagner turned his energies towards the creation of the first *Ring* festival. In March 1871 he informed Ludwig of his Bayreuth plan and, although far from pleased that Wagner had switched the venue from Munich, Ludwig accepted the decision as irrevocable. A visit to Bayreuth in April established that the Markgräfliches Opernhaus was unsuitable for staging the *Ring*, and so Wagner determined, there and then, to build a brand new theatre. Such an undertaking would, he realised, require substantial capital, and the next five years were to be spent on a

113

tireless quest for financial (and artistic) support for the scheme. The wheels were set in motion during a stay in Berlin later that April when, as well as enjoying an historic meeting with Bismarck, Wagner was able to discuss money matters with his newly chosen 'business manager', the gifted young pianist Carl Tausig. Wagner estimated the cost of building the theatre and organising the festival at 300,000 thalers, and Tausig devised the idea of raising the money by selling 1,000 'Patrons' Certificates' at 300 thalers each. After Tausig's untimely death a few months later, his scheme was developed further by Emil Heckel, a Mannheim music dealer, who inaugurated the still-flourishing Wagner Societies (Wagner-*Vereine*) to enable less well-off patrons to club together to buy certificates.

In default of his contractual obligations to Ludwig, on 12 May 1871 Wagner announced from Leipzig the first Bayreuth festival, set for 1873. Before this could happen, of course, the *Ring* had to be finished, and Wagner settled down at Tribschen to writing the composition sketch of *Götterdämmerung* Act II, which he completed in the amazingly short time of only four months (24 June-25 October 1871). Wagner found another willing supporter in the person of Friedrich Feustel, a banker and chairman of the Bayreuth town council who, after Wagner had written to him in November 1871, secured the agreement of his

Plan of a section of the
Bayreuth Festspielhaus,
1873.

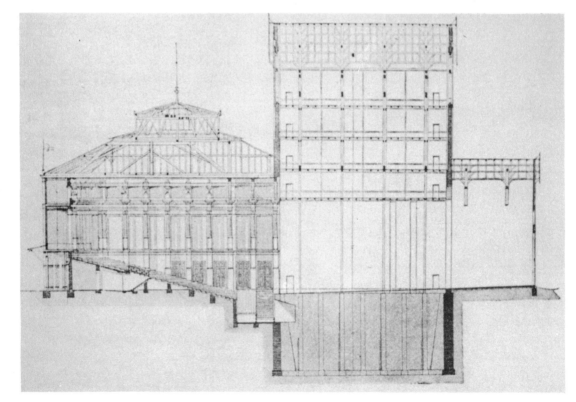

The Villa Wahnfried.

The *salon* at Wahnfried.

magnanimous fellow councillors to grant Wagner a suitable site for the building of his festival theatre. In February 1872, after starting *Götterdämmerung* Act III, Wagner travelled to Bayreuth again and set up a festival committee consisting of Feustel, the mayor Theodor Muncker and a local lawyer called Käfferlein. The site of the theatre – the Festspielhaus – was decided upon, and Wagner also acquired a plot of land on which to build his future house, Wahnfried.

Wagner and Cosima.

The composition sketch of *Götterdämmerung* was completed on 10 April 1872; and on 22 April, after six happy years, Wagner said goodbye to Tribschen for the last time, and moved·to Bayreuth. On 22 May 1872, Wagner's fifty-ninth birthday, a large crowd gathered in the pouring rain on the Grüne Hügel (Green Hill) overlooking the town to witness the laying of the foundation stone of the Festspielhaus. It was a solemn occasion, marred only by the absence of Wagner's old friend Liszt, with whom relations had

The Festspielhaus, Bayreuth.

cooled since Cosima's separation from Bülow. Ludwig, however, sent a telegram which, together with a poem by Wagner, was put in a casket and lowered into place together with the stone. The ceremony continued in the Markgräfliches Opernhaus, where Wagner made a speech and conducted a performance of Beethoven's Ninth Symphony, a work that he always claimed had played such a significant part in his musical development.

In November 1872 Wagner and Cosima set off on the first of their exhausting talent-spotting tours of Germany to look for singers, but the trip only confirmed what Wagner had always feared – that incompetence, especially amongst conductors, was rife in every area of opera. To add to Wagner's misery, the new year brought more bad news. The festival committee reported that insufficient numbers of Patrons' Certificates were being sold, and that even the Wagner Societies had raised far less money than anticipated. It was fast becoming painfully clear that, as always, Wagner's main problem was going to be a financial one; and the only solution at this time was for him to give a series of concerts

around the country, which brought in much-needed funds but put further strain on his already sorely-taxed state of health.

In August 1873 a party was held to celebrate the completion of the shell of Festspielhaus. However, Wagner was advised by the festival committee that if the building of the theatre was to continue, a loan would have to be secured from a wealthy (preferably royal) patron. Not one German prince had shown any inclination to support the festival and, in desperation, Wagner appealed to Ludwig for help; but the King was by this time involved in his own building schemes, and the plea was rejected. Faced with this disappointment, Wagner was obliged to tell the patrons of Bayreuth that the festival would not take place until 1875. In November 1873 Wagner again wrote to Ludwig (through the medium of the King's Court Secretary Düfflipp), but in January 1874 his request was once again turned down. After toying with an abortive plan to apply to the Kaiser for help, Wagner was faced with the dismal prospect of his cherished project collapsing in ruins; but then, on 25 January, good fortune

Caricature of Ludwig as
'King Lohengrin'.

intervened in the welcome form of a letter from Ludwig, who had had, amazingly, an abrupt change of heart. 'No, no, and no again! It shall not end like this,' wrote the King. 'Something must be done. Our plan must not be allowed to fail!'

In February 1874 a contract was drawn up between the festival committee and the Court Treasury guaranteeing a loan of 100,000 thalers, on condition that the income from the sale of Patrons' Certificates be repaid to the Treasury. In the end, the loan amounted to 216,152 marks (one thaler was worth approximately three marks) which was eventually paid back entirely by Wagner's heirs. Ludwig also gave Wagner 25,000 thalers to complete his new home, the Villa Wahnfried (translatable as 'peace from illusion'), into which the Wagner family moved on 28 April 1874. Wahnfried, which is now a museum, remained Wagner's home until his death, and became the temple of the new cult of Wagnerism which swept through Europe during the last two decades of the nineteenth century, and beyond, exerting its influence not just on music and opera, but on every sphere of the arts – an influence that ultimately was to have a far-reaching effect on the culture of the modern age.

Life at Wahnfried was a well-ordered affair, with domestic contentment and a rigid adherence to routine both essential factors in Wagner's ability to cope with the tremendous burden of work he had set himself. Each day was carefully planned: work on the scoring of *Götterdämmerung* in the morning, lunch with the children, then, in the afternoon, a leaf through the newspapers, an attack on the copious post-bag and the management of any festival

A gathering of Wagner's
friends and colleagues at
Wahnfried.

Hans Richter.

business, followed by a walk in the park with the children. After dinner, he and Cosima would settle down for an evening of reading or music-making, often in the company of the 'Nibelung Chancellery', a small group of young musicians engaged by Wagner to proof-read and copy out parts, and to assist in coaching the singers.

During 1874 Wagner, with Richter's help, was busy selecting and training the orchestra members and singers from all over Germany who would (for no fees) perform the first Bayreuth festival. Again the date was postponed, until 1876, to allow time for the complex preparations to be properly completed. The full score of *Götterdämmerung* was at last finished on 21 November 1874, amid constant interruptions, twenty-six years after Wagner first conceived the *Ring* in Dresden in 1848. Money for the building work on the Festspielhaus continued to be a problem, however, despite the King's loan, and during the first half of 1875 Wagner had to pay for it by giving yet more hated concert tours around Europe. His conducting fees also covered the cost of the

122

orchestral and stage rehearsals which began in the newly finished theatre in August 1875, when Wagner was able to hear for the first time the acoustical effect of the unique sunken orchestra pit, originally designed for Semper's ill-fated Munich theatre.

Wagner closely supervised all the rehearsals and helped coach the players in his inimitable style, singing the lines himself and directing with practised histrionics, while at the same time allowing each person the freedom to develop his or her own conception of the role. He had managed to amass some first-class singers in Bayreuth, including Franz Betz as Wotan, Albert Niemann as Siegmund, Georg Unger as Siegfried, and Amalie Materna as Brünnhilde. The scenery was done by the Brückner brothers of Coburg to designs by the painter Joseph Hoffmann; Richard Fricke was the choreographer, and Richter conducted. Rehearsals went well, but hopes of artistic success were overshadowed by the fact that the festival was still on an unsound financial footing. At the end of 1875 only 490 Patrons' Certificates had been sold – well short of the original target. In desperation he applied to Emperor Wilhelm I for a loan, but the request was politely turned down. In the end, despite other fund-raising efforts by Wagner, it was only after Ludwig agreed in June 1876 to suspend the repayments on the loan that the festival was able to proceed.

Full rehearsals of the *Ring* took place between June and August 1876, while last-minute work was being done on the building and the sets. The dress rehearsals were held between 6 and 9 August, and were attended by King Ludwig, who had slipped into Bayreuth at dead of night, and departed after *Götterdämmerung* in similar secretive fashion. It had been his first meeting with Wagner for eight years and, notwithstanding all the water that had flowed under the bridge, he left as enraptured as, when a boy, he had first sat trembling at that fateful performance of *Lohengrin* in Munich in 1861.

The festival at last began on 13 August 1876, in the presence of the Emperor – an historic occasion, as Wagner later noted, since 'for the first time emperors and princes had come to the artist'. There were three *Ring* cycles during August, all of which were a resounding success (although Wagner was less than happy with some of the performances). Ludwig was persuaded to return for the third cycle, joining a host of esteemed visitors from all over Europe. Among Wagner's many friends and admirers who made the pilgrimage to Bayreuth were the Wesendoncks and Judith Gautier, whose romantic attentions provided him with a welcome respite from the strains of the festival. Nietzsche, who had been a regular guest at Wahnfried, attended the rehearsals and the first cycle, but his health was rapidly deteriorating (he later went

Friedrich Nietzsche.

Wagner, *c.*1876.

insane) and the blinding headaches he suffered in Bayreuth added acute physical discomfort to the growing spiritual unease he was experiencing towards Wagner's art, which was soon to turn into bitter condemnation and hatred.

At the end of the festival the visitors departed, and Wagner, by now thoroughly exhausted, retired to Wahnfried to count the cost – both emotional and financial – of his immense undertaking. By a mixture of inspired organisation, prodigious hard work, sheer determination, and against all the odds, Wagner had managed to hold everything together and forge a great artistic triumph. But the prize had been won without the help of the German people, for whom the *Ring* had been created – and to add to his depression over what he saw as a betrayal of his efforts, he learned that the festival showed a deficit of nearly 150,000 marks, which put its whole future in serious jeopardy. In need of rest, Wagner took a touring holiday with Cosima and the children in Italy (where, in November 1876, on the seafront in Sorrento, he had his last meeting with Nietzsche); but Bayreuth was never far from his thoughts, and it was not long before he was again appealing to his loyal friend King Ludwig to rescue the festival from this latest crisis.

Left:
Act II, Scene 5 of *Die Walküre*. Siegmund is killed by Hunding while Sieglinde looks on helplessly.

125

10 Death in Venice

Final scene of *Parsifal*,
designed by Joukovsky for
1882 production.

After returning from Italy, Wagner began to formulate plans as to how the festival enterprise might be saved. His principal scheme was that the Munich opera should take over the running of the festival, but Ludwig was not keen on the suggestion; and besides, as Secretary Düfflipp pointed out to him, 'because of His Majesty's building activities, the demands on the resources of the Cabinet Treasury are such as to exclude expenditure of funds for other purposes'. With the prospects for Bayreuth once again

Final scene of *Parsifal*, designed by Joukovsky for 1882 production.

Wagner in London, 1877.

looking bleak, Wagner sought solace in his creative work, as he often did in times of stress. Between February and April 1877 he wrote the prose draft (the second, the first having been written in Munich in 1865) and the libretto of *Parsifal*, his last opera. Wagner was anxious, however, to show his Bayreuth friends that he was determined to help in any way he could to reduce the deficit and, after completing *Parsifal*, he decided to accept an invitation to conduct a series of twenty concerts at the Royal Albert Hall in London, where he arrived on 1 May.

Wagner had considerable misgivings about revisiting London after the miserable experience of his last stay in 1855, and it soon became clear that his anxieties were at least partly justified. The concert agents, Hodge & Essex, had originally assured him that an excellent profit could be expected from ticket sales in the 10,000 capacity hall, but owing to their inexperience they had both greatly overestimated the demand and overlooked the fact that 2,000 of these seats belonged to subscribers and could not be sold to the general public. As a result, the twenty concerts had to be reduced to eight and, although they were a huge artistic success, in the end Wagner received only £700 and had to pay the singers' fees out of his own pocket. As a small consolation, in contrast to his

Royal Albert Hall, London.

earlier visits Wagner was treated like a celebrity. He was received by Queen Victoria at Windsor Castle, and in the course of being wined and dined was introduced to some of the major artistic personalities of the day, including Robert Browning, George Eliot, William Morris and Edward Burne-Jones.

In financial terms, however, the month-long trip was a thorough disappointment, with the proceeds only scratching the surface of the Bayreuth deficit. To keep the most insistent creditors at bay, Wagner provided 50,000 marks from his private savings, but things now seemed so hopeless that he seriously

127

Cosima Wagner, 1879.

Wagner, London 1877.

contemplated emigrating to the United States, never again to return to Germany. He wrote despondently to Friedrich Feystel in June 1877:

My work will be performed everywhere, and people will flock to see it – but no one will come to Bayreuth. I can only blame the town to the extent that it was I who chose it. Yet I did so with a great idea: with the support of the nation I wanted to create something entirely new and independent to which the town would owe its importance – a kind of Washington of Art. I expected too much from the upper echelons of our society.

Although horrified by Wagner's threat to emigrate to the United States, Ludwig was still reluctant to step in and save the 'Bayreuth Idea'. On 15 September 1877 Wagner addressed the delegates from all the Wagner Societies who assembled in the Festspielhaus to be told the fate of the festival. They were, he said, 'back at the beginning again', though on a more optimistic note

128

Wagner outlined his plan for the establishment of a music school in Bayreuth, where musicians would be trained to perform in the true 'German style'. The plan, as with the one for Munich, was never realised. Later that month he began the composition of Act I of *Parsifal* (and an amorous though short-lived correspondence with Judith Gautier), but by the beginning of 1878 it became clear that the outstanding debt – which stood at 98,634 marks – could not be ignored for much longer. With legal proceedings looming, Cosima, fearful of the effect such a catastrophe would have on Wagner's creativity – and his declining state of health – took the bold step of writing to Ludwig herself begging for his assistance. Her plea had the desired effect, and on 31 March 1878 an agreement was signed between Wagner and the Treasury whereby the debt would be discharged by a loan, repayable at five per cent interest, and Wagner would be paid a ten per cent royalty each time any of his works were performed in Munich.

129

Cartoon of Wagner, Liszt and Bülow.

Cartoon of Wagner by Charles Lyall, London 1877.

With his money worries removed, Wagner was able to concentrate on the composition sketch of *Parsifal*, which he completed in April 1879. The subject-matter of *Parsifal* has often been linked with some of the more disturbing philosophical ideas which Wagner vigorously expounded in the last years of his life concerning race, religion and the regeneration of European culture, which he saw as decadent and corrupt. The principal vehicle for these theories and doctrines was the *Bayreuther Blätter*, a monthly journal founded in January 1878 to which Wagner contributed a series of articles – all of which were eagerly received by a growing number of followers, who would gather at Wahnfried to hear the Master's views on everything from vivisection to the 'Jewish problem'. In these articles, Wagner gave unrestrained expression to his rampant anti-semitism (which he attempted to rationalise with quasi-theological reasoning), attacking what he saw as the false and pernicious religion of Judaism, which had subverted the true Christian faith, and even advocating a return to a vegetable diet as a prerequisite of mankind's hoped-for regeneration.

Wagner was still furious at the lack of support he had received from the German people for the Bayreuth festival. This disappointment undoubtedly served to intensify his belief that a growing cultural malaise had gripped the nation, for which the Jews, who were popularly seen by the German bourgeoisie as having an invidious influence on society, should be held responsible to a large degree. In one of the most controversial articles, *Heroism and Christianity* (1881), Wagner adopted the racial theories of the French writer Arthur de Gobineau (with whom he had some lengthy discussions in Venice in 1880), who argued that the superior Aryan race was being corrupted by interbreeding with inferior stock – in Wagner's mind, the Jews. Analogies between these ideas of racial purity and, for example, the Grail brotherhood in *Parsifal* are clearly there to be drawn. Wagner characteristically believed the solution to the Jewish influence in German culture lay in the redemptive power of (his) art, and never advocated more direct action (in 1880 he refused to sign an anti-Jewish petition to the Reichstag, saying 'I have nothing at all to do with the present anti-semitic movement'). It was not until this century that his line of thought in the *Bayreuther Blätter* essays was taken to its terrible conclusion, as Hitler and the Nazis sought an all too real and final solution to the 'Jewish problem'.

By the end of 1879 the decline in Wagner's health had become serious enough for him to leave Germany for the more congenial climate of Italy, where he was to spend much of his time during the

Meilhac as Kundry, in *Parsifal*.

131

last three years of his life. In January 1880 he and his family moved into the Villa Angri on the Bay of Naples, where he concentrated his energies on the scoring of *Parsifal*, which he had started in Bayreuth in August 1879. As well as enjoying the invigorating Italian sunshine, Wagner had also become increasingly disillusioned with Bismarck and the Empire which, he felt, had not lived up to its early promise and was shamelessly promoting militarism at the expense of cultural progress. He now believed – and hoped – that the future belonged to socialism, which he saw as essential if attitudes were to change and national support for his festival was ever to be forthcoming.

Wagner remained in Italy for most of 1880, not returning to Bayreuth until October. Guests at the Villa Angri included the philosopher Heinrich von Stein, who joined the family as Siegfried's tutor; the composer Engelbert Humperdinck; and the young Russian painter Paul von Joukovsky, who was to design the scenery and costumes for *Parsifal*, and who became Wagner's close companion in his remaining years. On a visit to Amalfi together, they visited the Palazzo Rufolo on the gulf of Salerno, where Wagner found the model for Klingsor's magic garden in Act II of *Parsifal*. In July 1880 Wagner and family left Naples and travelled further north to Siena, where he rented a large villa just outside the city. There he was visited by Liszt, with whom he had

The Temple of the Grail from *Parsifal*, a painting based on Joukovsky's design.

132

Liszt.

at last become reconciled, and completed the fourth (and, as it turned out, the final) part of his autobiography, *Mein Leben*, which took him up to the time of his summons to Munich in 1864. Also while in Siena, Wagner visited the cathedral, whose imposing interior so moved him that he instructed Joukovsky to make a series of sketches, which were used as the basis of the first sets for the Temple of the Grail in Acts I and III of *Parsifal*.

On the way back to Bayreuth, Wagner stopped off for a few weeks in Munich where, on 12 November 1880, he conducted a private performance of the *Parsifal* prelude for Ludwig, who sat alone in the royal box. This was to be their last meeting. Ludwig was retreating further and further into his dream world of legends and castles, and his mental health continued to deteriorate rapidly until, in 1886, he was found, along with another man, drowned in Lake Starnberg. In May 1881 Wagner travelled to Berlin for the first *Ring* production there, organised by Angelo Neumann, the director of the Leipzig Opera, whose own touring company later contributed greatly to the spread of Wagner's fame throughout Europe during the remainder of the nineteenth century. Now suffering from severe chest pains, in November Wagner headed south again to Sicily; and it was there, in Palermo on 13 January 1882, that he finally completed the full score of *Parsifal*. Two days

later he had his portrait painted by Renoir (which he said made him look like a 'Protestant minister'). After spending the spring in Palermo, he returned to Bayreuth in May to prepare for the next festival.

Wagner called *Parsifal* a 'Consecrated Festival Drama', although it is misleading to think of it, as Nietzsche did, as fundamentally a religious, Christian work. In fact, pagan, Buddhist and Schopenhauerian ideas, as well as Christian elements, are incorporated into the *Parsifal* poem; and essentially Wagner was concerned, as in his other music dramas, not with expressing a particular ideology, but with revealing the unconscious world of thought and feeling through myths and symbols. As he explained in one of his *Bayreuther Blätter* essays, *Religion and Art* (1880):

One could say that, when religion becomes artificial, it is left to art to save the essence of religion by apprehending the value of its mythic symbols, which religion would have us take literally, so that the deep, hidden truth in these symbols can be revealed through their ideal representation.

134

Before the festival started, Wagner dissolved the Society of Patrons, which had shown itself unable to come up with the necessary finance; so that admission was now open to the general public, who paid for tickets in the normal way. The première of *Parsifal* took place in the Festspielhaus on 26 July 1882, conducted by Hermann Levi, a Jew, whom Wagner was (reluctantly) obliged to accept under the terms of his 1878 agreement with Ludwig, by which the company of the Munich Hoftheater was, at the King's insistence, placed at his disposal. (Paradoxically, many of the musicians who worked closely with Wagner were Jews, despite the fact that he never tried to hide his anti-semitism, and often maliciously vilified them.) There were sixteen performances of *Parsifal* in all, at the last of which, on 29 August, Wagner took the baton from Levi during the transformation scene in Act III and conducted the work to the end. Although saddened that Ludwig did not attend, Wagner could take ample consolation in the knowledge that the 1882 festival had been a great success, both artistically and financially, with the profits from the ticket sales making a festival the following year a viable possibility.

The preparations for *Parsifal* had however taken their toll on Wagner's health, and the pains in his chest had worsened as a result of his exertions. In September, therefore, in need of some Italian sunshine, he moved with his family to Venice, where they rented a floor of the Palazzo Vendramin, overlooking the Grand Canal. Wagner lived quietly in Venice, spending his time reading, writing an essay for the *Bayreuther Blätter* on *Parsifal*, and taking

The Palazzo Vendramin, Venice.

136

gondola trips along the canals with Cosima. In November Liszt arrived at the Palazzo Vendramin for a two-month stay, during which time he wrote the funereal piano piece *La lugubre gondola* and discussed with Wagner the latter's idea for composing a symphony. This plan was never realised, but Wagner's re-awakened interest in purely orchestral music did find a romantic outlet on Christmas Eve 1882 when, to celebrate Cosima's birthday, he organised and conducted a performance of his C major Symphony, which he had written in Leipzig fifty years before.

On the evening of 12 February 1883, after Joukovsky had made a sketch of his face as he sat reading, Wagner stayed up long after everybody else had retired, playing to himself the Rhinemaidens' lament from the end of *Das Rheingold* on the piano. The following morning, after rising late, he went to his study to continue the essay he had started a few days before, *Concerning the Feminine in the Human*, which detailed his views on love, marriage and sexual

Alberich and the
Rhinemaidens in *Das
Rheingold*. 'Save the gold!'

137

Programme of *Tristan and Isolde* benefit performance.

equality. When Joukovsky arrived for lunch at around two o'clock, he found Cosima in tears (possibly following an argument with Wagner earlier that morning), playing Schubert's *Lob der Tränen* on the piano. Wagner sent a message asking to be excused the meal, as he felt unwell. Soon afterwards the maid was alerted by a groan coming from his room and she found him at his desk, struggling with pain, his unfinished essay lying in front of him. Cosima came immediately and the doctor was summoned, but there was nothing to be done. He had suffered a fatal heart attack and died at around three-thirty that afternoon in Cosima's arms.

The next day Wagner's death mask was made by the sculptor Augusto Benvenuti, and on 16 February his body was taken in a gondola to the railway station, from where it was transported to Bayreuth. Cosima, who had clung to her husband's body for over twenty-four hours, was so grief-stricken and so weak through fasting, that for a while her life also seemed in jeopardy. 'Fortunate century that saw such a genius rise from its midst,' Ludwig had written after seeing *Götterdämmerung*; and the countless tributes and messages that poured into Bayreuth from all over Europe were clear evidence of the inestimable impact Wagner's art had had on the imagination of his age. On the morning of 18 February, the funeral procession made its way through the crowd-lined streets to Wagner's final resting place; and at a private ceremony attended only by Cosima and a few close friends, his body was interred in the tomb in the garden of Wahnfried, at peace at last from all illusion.

Left:
Wagner's funeral procession, Bayreuth.

Right:
Cosima at Wagner's tomb.

RICHARD WAGNER

Completed Stage Works

	Composed	First Performance
Die Feen	1834	Munich 1888
Das Liebesverbot	1835	Magdeburg 1836
Rienzi, the Last of the Tribunes	1840	Dresden 1842
Der fliegende Holländer	1841	Dresden 1843
Tannhäuser	1843-45	Dresden 1845
Lohengrin	1847-48	Weimar 1850
Das Rheingold	1853-54	Munich 1869
Die Walküre	1854-56	Munich 1870
Siegfried	1856-71 (Gap of 12 years between Acts II and III	Bayreuth 1876
Tristan und Isolde	1857-59	Munich 1865
Die Meistersinger von Nürnberg	1862-67	Munich 1868
Götterdämmerung	1869-74	Bayreuth 1876
Parsifal	1877-82	Bayreuth 1882

Bibliography

Barth, Mack and Voss. *Wagner: A Documentary Study* (London 1975)

Burbidge, Peter and Sutton, Richard (eds). *The Wagner Companion* (London 1979)

Chancellor, John. *Wagner* (London 1978)

Culshaw, John. *Reflections on Wagner's Ring* (London 1976)

Dalhaus, Carl and Deathridge, John. *The New Grove Wagner* (London 1984)

Donington, Robert. *Wagner's Ring and its Symbols* (London 1963)

Fischer-Dieskau, Dietrich. *Wagner and Nietzsche* (London 1978)

Gutman, Robert. *Richard Wagner: The Man, His Mind and His Music* (London 1968)

Gregor-Dellin, Martin. *Richard Wagner: His Life, His Work, His Century* (London 1983)

Magee, Bryan. *Aspects of Wagner* (London 1968)

Mann, Thomas. *Pro and Contra Wagner* (London 1985)

Newman, Ernest. *The Life of Richard Wagner* (4 vols, London 1933)
— *Wagner Nights* (London 1949)

Porter, Andrew. *Richard Wagner: The Ring* (translation, London 1976)

Skelton, Geoffrey. *Wagner at Bayreuth* (London 1976)

Westernhagen, Curt von. *Wagner: A Biography* (Cambridge 1978)

Index

*Page numbers in **bold** refer to illustrations*